Advance Praise
Off Your Rocker

"There are few things more comforting than the warmth of a grandparent's heart. Off Your Rocker gives practical advice for staying connected with your grandkids...while building loving relationships and happy memories. Start reading it today!"

—Dr. Charles Fay, author of *Love and Logic Magic for Early Childhood: Practical Parenting from Birth to Six Years* and cofounder of The Love and Logic Institute

"As a new grandparent, I found this book to be rich with inspiration and full of great ideas! Keep this helpful resource nearby as a guide for creating deep and lasting relationships with your grandchildren!"

—**Kay Allenbaugh**, author of the nationally bestselling *Chocolate for a Woman's Soul* series

"As a grandparent with grandchildren scattered from coast to coast, I'm always searching for good ways to build strong relationships with them all. Fortunately, Off Your Rocker makes the job simple. It's filled from cover to cover with hundreds of great ways to have fun with grandchildren."

—**Dick Hodgson**, author and grandfather of six, West Chester, Pennsylvania

"Off Your Rocker is a must-read for all grandparents! As an educator and grandparent I have come to realize the importance of leaving a legacy for your children and grandchildren. This book is filled with wonderful suggestions and creative ideas, as well as sweet remembrances of grandparents, to inspire us to be actively involved in the lives of our grandchildren."

—**Karen Watts**, elementary school principal; grandmother of two

"I laughed and I cried at the wonderful stories in this book, but—more importantly—I was inspired and motivated by literally hundreds of fun ways to build relationships (and memories) with my grandchildren. I couldn't put it down."

—**Sue Kirby**, humorist and author of *Men's Secret Camp*; grandmother of ten

parent's guide press

Off Your Rocker!

The Ultimate Guide for Grandparents

**Nancy Rosenberg
& Judy Haire**

los angeles, california  **parent's**
guide
press

Off Your Rocker!
The Ultimate Guide for Grandparents

ISBN: 1-931199-35-3

© 2003 Mars Publishing, Inc.

All rights reserved. No part of this publication may be reproduced, stored in a retrieval system or transmitted in any form by any means electronic, mechanical, photocopying, recording, or otherwise, except for brief extracts for the purpose of review, without written permission of the publisher and copyright holder.

Mars Publishing and the Mars Publishing Logo, Parent's Guide and the Parent's Guide logo are trademarks of Mars Publishing, Inc. The author and Mars Publishing have tried to make the information in this book as accurate as possible. We accept no responsibility for any loss, injury, or inconvenience sustained by anyone using this book.

Edwin E. Steussy, CEO and Publisher
Dianne Tangel-Cate, Project Editor
Michael P. Duggan, Graphic Artist

PO Box 461730
Los Angeles CA 90046

**parent's
guide
press**

Off Your Rocker!
The Ultimate Guide for Grandparents

Contents

Off Your Rocker!
The Ultimate Guide for Grandparents

Contents

Off Your Rocker!
The Ultimate Guide for Grandparents

Contents

Off Your Rocker!
The Ultimate Guide for Grandparents

Contents

DEDICATION

For Blanche and Major Collins (Meemaw and Gong Gong), who have demonstrated through the years how to grandparent with humor, love, and devotion, and in memory of Nana, Bompy, Mimi, and Bill. We miss you every day.

"So many things we love are you, I can't seem to explain except by little things, but flowers and beautiful handmade things—small stitches. So much of our reading and thinking, so many sweet customs... It is all you. I hadn't realized it before. This is so vague, but do you see, dear Grandma? I want to thank you."

—Anne Morrow Lindbergh,
from *Bring Me a Unicorn*

Introduction

There's no secret to being a successful grandparent, yet success in this area eludes many. In an era of X-Box, rollerblades, and Britney Spears, many grandparents feel alienated, left behind, and helpless to form and sustain long-term, successful relationships with their mysterious grandchildren.

What many grandparents fail to realize, however, is that their presence in the lives of their grandchildren is needed now more than ever. Divorce is rampant, drugs are readily available, and casual teen and preteen sex is epidemic. Latchkey kids find themselves lonely, bored, and unsupervised. If there ever was a time for grandparents to confidently stride into the lives of their grandchildren, it is now.

Off Your Rocker! is chock full of innovative, interesting ideas for connecting to babies, children, and teens. There are also specific chapters to help deal with some of the more difficult issues that grandparents may face, such as grandchildren in trouble, long-distance grandparenting, and dealing with illness and loss.

In this book, you'll find practical suggestions for where to take kids, what to do with them, how to talk to them, and how to build memories that your grandchildren will cherish for a lifetime. We've interviewed kids, parents, grandparents, family psychologists, ministers, and teachers and included their ideas. After reading this book, you'll have all the tools you need to connect with your grandkids and build strong, satisfying, and lasting relationships.

Off Your Rocker!
The Ultimate Guide for Grandparents

Introduction

Why This Book Is Different

Most books on grandparenting are written from the perspective of the grandparent. While there's nothing wrong with this approach, it provides a decidedly flat perspective. This book is written from the perspectives of a parent and a grandparent, with lots of input from probably the most reliable source when it comes to this issue: kids.

We firmly believe that grandparents can be invaluable sources of wisdom and learning for their grandchildren, and here you'll find hundreds of ideas for communicating that wisdom.

Before we delve into the thick of grandparenting and what you can do to hone your skills, let's first look at a few of the demographics of grandparents. While previous generations tended to view grandparents as a doddering group who showed its age, a wave of youthful, energetic baby boomers is rapidly changing that perception.

Did You Know That...

1. About one-third of American adults are grandparents. There are currently 70 million grandparents in the United States. With more and more baby boomers approaching grandparent age, this number is expected to swell to over 115 million by 2010. The average age of first-time grandparents is forty-seven.

2. Fifty-nine percent of grandparents have grandchildren in the eight to twelve age group; 57 percent have grandkids ages four to seven.

3. Today's grandparents have higher levels of education and income than their predecessors, and they take a more active role in their grandkids' education and cultural enrichment. They also participate more in arts and culture themselves. The number of grandparents attending at least one music or dance performance a year, for example, has increased 227 percent since 1988.

Introduction

4. More than 6 percent of all children under age eighteen in the United States are growing up in grandparent-headed households. (That's an increase of 30 percent since 1990.)

5. With parents working longer hours and committing to overly busy schedules, many grandparents now assume a greater role in the lives of their grandchildren. But while spending time with grandma and grandpa used to mean visiting them at home, today it's more likely to mean taking an educational day trip or going to a sporting or entertainment event together.

6. Because Americans are living longer, healthier lives and often marrying more than once, kids today have more grandparents than ever before. They also have more great-grandparents. In the past thirty years, the number of great-grandparents actively involved in their great-grandchildren's lives has increased tenfold.

7. As a group, grandparents now spend more than $30 billion a year on their grandkids, a two-fold increase over what was spent a decade ago.

8. It's estimated that grandparents account for almost 17 percent of toy sales in the U.S., with the fifty-five to sixty-four age group spending more per capita on toys than the twenty-five to forty-four age group. Yet today's grandparents are even more interested in spending money on activities they can do with their grandchildren.

9. Grandparents traveling with their grandkids accounted for one in every five trips taken with children in the year 2000. Six million Americans reported vacationing with their grandchildren in a typical month.

10. "Grandtravel," grandparents traveling with grandchildren, is becoming so popular that tour operators, hotels, cruise lines, and even elder hostels have developed programs and promotions tailored to this market.

Sources: AARP, American Demographics, NDP Group, Bureau of Labor Statistics, Travel Industry Association of America, Roper Organization, Museum Marketing.

Chapter One

Realize the Potential

"To help the young soul redeem defeat by new thought and firm action, this, though not easy, is the work of divine man."
—Ralph Waldo Emerson

When your now-grown child first announces that a baby is on the way, and when your son or daughter places that precious newborn bundle in your arms, you'll likely be overcome with emotion. Overwhelming love and gratitude are hallmarks of those once-in-a-lifetime moments, but you are likely to feel other emotions, too.

Becoming a grandparent changes the way you see yourself and the way others perceive you. Your idea of being a grandparent may be accompanied by visions of an older generation, gray-haired women baking cookies and retired men sitting by a lake. One newly divorced older woman told her married son, only halfway joking, "Don't you dare make me a grandparent yet! I can't be a grandmother and go out on dates!"

Once that first grandchild arrives, you are suddenly faced with the realities of the life cycle, of birth and death, of aging and becoming part of an older generation.

However, along with these changing perceptions in identity comes an opportunity to reinvent yourself. A new relative has joined the family, and you get to present yourself in any way you want. You get to decide if you want to be wise Barbara Bush or funky Goldie Hawn, dignified Dick Clark or winking Sean Connery…the possibilities are endless!

Realize the Potential

What Kind of Grandparent Will You Be?

In her delightful gift book *Grandmothers*, Helen Exley describes how the role of grandparents shifts and evolves with time:

"In all the old stories grandmothers taught their little children to crochet and knit and sew a fine seam. They existed in cozy kitchens, warm and fragrant with the smell of spice buns and newly baked bread and freshly laundered sheets.

"A dream. Comforting—but a dream. For nowadays Grandma is probably in jeans and baggy sweater and can't sew to save her life. Her hair can be any shade in the spectrum—and she irons as little as she can. However, she's handy with a spade—and last week she shifted the furniture around and stripped and papered the living room entirely on her own.

"She sometimes knocks together a batch of scones when her grandchildren come to call—but is just as likely to have gotten them from the supermarket. For she's busy, she's got her art class and her course in car maintenance. If, of course, she's not running a business or writing a novel or organizing a protest or preparing to sail around the world.

"But she's just as much a grandma. She'll give the grandchildren a good grounding in politics and healthy eating. And how to mend a fuse. And how to make a genuine pizza. Her hugs are just as loving—and she's just as good at stories and secrets—and having a quick word with dad."

—Pam Brown, from *Grandmothers* by Helen Exley

What kind of grandparent will you be? Part of what can make the idea of being a grandparent unsettling is the lack of firm societal rules and directions. Psychologists talk about the grandparent relationship being idiosyncratic rather than normative; there are no clear rights and responsibilities to being a grandparent. And every family is different.

Off Your Rocker!
The Ultimate Guide for Grandparents

Chapter One

It is at this juncture that many first-time grandparents feel a sense of self-doubt that borders on confusion. What should I do? How will I be perceived? Will my grandchild love me as much as he loves the other grandparents? Can I help my child with parenting responsibilities without becoming authoritarian? Can I spoil my grandchild? What if I don't do it right?

When first-time grandparents reach this point of general anxiety, they need to take a deep breath and relax. Know that eventually you will find your rhythm and hit your stride. What type of grandparent you'll turn out to be isn't the important question. Just like we all have different personalities and parenting styles, we each develop our own style of grandparenting.

Here, though, is the important question: *Will you be an active participant in the lives of your grandchildren?* Unlike the relationship you had with your children, you may now have a choice. Unless you are the primary caregiver, you can call your grandchildren once a week, once a month, or never at all. You can see them whenever it's convenient, every chance you get, or once a year during the holidays. The choice is yours, and grandchildren somehow understand this intuitively. If you choose to be less involved in their lives, most grandchildren accept the situation without complaint. "That's just the way grandma is."

But here's the thing: when the quality of the relationship is so optional, it's easier to let it slide. If you have grandchildren who live far away, this becomes even more of a reality. And, unlike adult relationships, whether or not you have a relationship with your grandchild is not equally determined by both parties involved. Your grandchild most likely won't be the one initiating contact, picking up the phone to call, or sending you nice little surprises in the mail. No, the burden of contact lies with the grandparent, especially when the grandchildren are young.

Realize the Potential

Mary Jo's Story

"When I was young, my grandparents played a very important part in my life. My parents were divorced, and I rarely saw my father. My mom had to work long hours to support my brother and me, so we spent a lot of time at my grandparents' house. I also had a hard time in school. I had a hard time learning, was continually picked on by other kids, and had very few friends.

"My grandparents had seven children and many grandchildren. It would have been very easy to feel like just another grandchild, but my grandpa didn't let that happen. Every day after work he would sit at the dining room table and work on his crossword puzzle. From where he sat, he could see our car when we pulled into the driveway. He would wait to hear the back door open and then he would call out, 'Is that my fickle frivolous woman?' And as I was running through the kitchen I would respond, 'And I'm smart, too.' I would give him a big hug and kiss and he would laugh and tell me that I was the smartest girl he knew.

"This was a cute ritual when I was five and even when I was ten, but when I reached my teen years it seemed very childish. I was working very hard at growing up too fast and didn't have time for Grandpa's childish game. When I would come over with a friend or, even worse, a boyfriend, I would try to ignore him and hide in the kitchen, but he wouldn't give up until I responded. Every time I would go over to his house, I would wish he would just stop. One day he did. When I was eighteen my grandpa passed away. Now every time I think of him I just wish I could tell him how special our game made me feel. I wish I could tell him that when the kids at school would tell me how stupid I was I would say to myself, 'My grandpa thinks I am smart.' I wish that I could tell him that whenever a family member calls me, I know that they understand the special bond that Grandpa and I had. I wish I could go back, but I can't. So, I go forward and try to pass on the love, acceptance, and encouragement that my grandpa blessed me with as a child."

—Contributed by Mary Jo Brooks

Chapter One

Conscious Grandparenting

You can make great strides in your relationships with your grandchildren by making it a practice to slow down and savor the time you have together. This conscious grandparenting, or grandparenting with awareness, means that you'll be sitting up straight, metaphorically speaking, and paying attention. You won't have to spend vast amounts of time with your progeny in order to build strong, healthy relationships if the time you do spend with them is spent well.

When spending time with the grandkids is on the agenda, take a few minutes before you get together and remember the age-old adage, "Anything worth doing is worth doing well." Children and teens today are buffeted by a host of challenging and potentially disastrous social pressures and temptations. Remind yourself that your role as a source of strength, love, and moral guidance should never be underestimated.

Realize, too, that in your grandchildren you have a second chance, an opportunity to rectify the mistakes you may have made as a parent. Did you rush through your own children's youth, fretting over spilled milk and a house in disarray and neglecting to appreciate the wonder, the humor, the entertainment value of small children?

It doesn't matter if you're a ninety-year-old geriatric marvel who regularly makes the front page of the local newspaper because of the marathons you run, or a fifty-five-year-old invalid who has had an unfortunate affliction with a long-term illness. You don't have to be in tip-top physical or mental shape in order to be an effective grandparent. All you have to have is a desire and willingness to be a part of your grandchildren's lives. It's that simple.

Realize the Potential

Why the Grandparent/Grandchild Relationship Is Key

Children know intuitively that there are some things that they just can't talk to mom or dad about. Their parents are too close and have invested too much in their kids to be objective. A close relationship with a grandparent can provide the perfect opportunity to share ideas or thoughts about difficult issues or concerns.

Grandparents also have the advantage of a long-term perspective. They tend to be less flustered by difficult issues or conversations; after all, they've been in this situation before, and they considered these issues for the first time many years ago. From a youth's perspective, conversations that touch on identity and morality can be much easier to have with a caring, listening grandparent.

"I have angels on my ceiling in my room. I painted them with my grandma. At night we sing about angels watching over me, over and over again. You can't get tired of that song when you are all snuggly with someone you love."

—Hannah P., seven years old
(from *Angels Among Us* by Phil Smart)

Chapter One
Parents Need Help

The demands of continuous care that are placed on parents today almost guarantee that parents will fail, at least to some extent, to be totally present for their children. Many parents now are dealing with marital strife, divorce, job uncertainty, and financial straits. Over 30 percent of children today under the age of eighteen live with a single parent. Times are hard; this is where you step in.

The degree to which you will be able to help your children with their children depends on several factors, including distance, your relationship with your child's spouse, and finances. Maybe you can best help by babysitting one or two afternoons a week after school, or maybe what is really needed is an occasional check or home-cooked meal. Your efforts to help your kids will be much more effective if you stand back and try to see objectively what it is they need the most.

There's a definite upside to helping out with your children's children that goes beyond the obvious. Solid grandparenting will do more than just develop your relationships with your grandchildren: It may improve the relationship you have with your children, too. Even though you may have your differences, when your children see the love and devotion you have toward their children, it engenders feelings of love, warmth, and gratitude.

So, then, what are some practical ways you can help your children?

- Offer to babysit one evening a week at a predetermined time. This might allow your son or daughter to make plans with their spouse for an evening out and will give them something to look forward to on a consistent basis; in turn, this could result in their having unwavering good feelings toward you, which is always a good thing!

Realize the Potential

- Have your grandchildren come and see you. If you live nearby, you can pick them up or the parents can drop them off. If you live far away, you can make plans in advance for the kids to spend some quality, uninterrupted, alone time with you each summer. The point is that while you are building relationships with your grandchildren, you are also giving their parents a break.

- Develop a few rituals with your grandchildren that can take pressure off of parents at critical times. For example, offer to take the grandchildren shopping during the holidays.

- Some grandparents find that they are in a strong position to be able to help their kids financially. While this is risky business and the subject should be handled with care, you may find that financial aid is a wonderful way to truly help your kids in the area they need it most.

- Offer moral support. A well-timed phone call to your son or daughter (or son- or daughter-in-law) "just to say hi and tell you what a great job I think you're doing" can be of tremendous value. No one completely outgrows the need for or appreciation of their parents' approval.

Finally, there is freedom in knowing that, although time spent with young children can be exhausting, grandparents have the unique opportunity to enjoy their progeny in small doses. You can play with your grandchildren, spend time with them, cuddle and console and talk and cook and explore, and then, when you're exhausted and they are tired and cranky, you can give them back! You can help parents when they need it most, but your commitment need not be permanent. Help out when you can, and rest assured that your efforts will be most appreciated.

Chapter One

One couple who rarely got to see their daughter, son-in-law, and grandsons—even though they lived just forty-five minutes away—had an inspired idea. "I knew my daughter was tired from working at the end of the day, so one day I offered to make and bring dinner to their house," says Bonnie. "It was on a Thursday, and I made things simple. A casserole, salad, paper plates. We had such a great time! On the way home, as my husband and I were talking about how much fun we had, my daughter called me and said the exact same thing. So now we have a Thursday night ritual. We make dinner and take it to their house. My daughter gets a break, and we get to spend time with all of them. It has become the highlight of my week!"

The Flip Side: Respecting the Wishes of the Parents

While you're busy trying to figure out how to help out with the grandkids, take great care not to undermine the thoughts, feelings, or desires of the parents. Ultimately it is the parents who hold the keys to your grandkids. If you want to enjoy the grandkids, you have to respect the wishes of the parents.

This can be a difficult concept to grasp for grandparents who are suddenly faced with the prospect of their children having the final word in a matter, but it's a necessary step in developing a harmonious family pattern of inter-relating, especially when grandchildren are involved.

Your efforts to reinforce what parents are trying to teach are key. If your daughter is in the middle of potty training her three-year-old, for example, you will win no points if you keep the toddler for a week and let the potty lessons slide, reasoning that "he's only little once; his parents can train him once he's back home."

Realize the Potential

If you instead make an effort to reinforce whatever lessons the parents are trying to instill, you win points on many levels: the parents are thrilled that their parenting efforts haven't been thwarted or delayed, and the kids themselves are reassured. Their world has stayed pretty much consistent. If mom and dad don't allow PG movies, for example, then do yourself a favor and maintain the ban consistently while the kids are in your care.

Another tip: have a quick conversation with the parents before you spend time with the grandkids and find out what the current issues are. Is seven-year-old Sara pushing the envelope and tending toward a smart mouth? Is nine-year-old Luke having trouble being accepted by his peers? Is two-year-old Angie being overly aggressive on the playground? Find out what the issues are ahead of time, then talk to the parents briefly about how they want you to approach them.

Coming to Terms with Imperfection

There are many grandparents who enjoy basking in ideal family scenarios in which their child is grown, married to a dear, and holds down a solid, well-paying job. They attend church regularly and have plenty of time and money before children even enter the picture. Once they do have children, the kids are smart, healthy, and well behaved. They live nearby, so the grandparents get to see the grandchildren whenever they want. Everything is sweetness and light.

There are legions more grandparents who are faced with grandparenting scenarios that fall somewhat outside of the range of the ideal. Perhaps your child is dealing with an out-of-wedlock pregnancy. You may think your child is too young to have children of his or her own. Perhaps the pregnancy has interrupted high school or college plans. Maybe your child's partner somehow doesn't measure up. Maybe they live too far away, so you won't be able to see the grandchildren as often as you would like.

Chapter One

Like most other types of relationships, the grandparent relationship is fraught with peril. There are a lot of factors that weigh in and a lot of things can go wrong. Maybe someone is sick. Maybe it's your child or grandchild. Maybe it's you.

As grandchildren get older, a whole host of potential catastrophes loom on the horizon. The challenge, then, is not to be cowed or intimidated by these very real circumstances, but to meet the challenges head on—with an awareness of what may be a less-than-ideal circumstance and a determination to make the best of it and to contribute to the family in a meaningful way.

The sooner you can let go of preconceived notions of the way things should be, the sooner you'll be on your way to healthier, happier relationships with your brood. If your child's marriage has failed, for example, you'll be much more helpful if you focus on practical ways to help your child, as opposed to dwelling on what went wrong and assigning blame.

Choose to Participate

A very busy, active retired couple, John and Sara once found themselves in a grandparenting quandary. They had forgotten to call their grandson on his birthday, and their son called in a huff that night, "Aren't you forgetting something?"

The couple had four grandchildren and another one on the way. Some of the grandkids lived just a few hours away, and others lived across the country. The couple found themselves feeling overwhelmed by the responsibilities of "all these grandkids."

"We've just decided that we're terrible grandparents," John told his son one night on the phone. "Don't expect much from us. We're too busy and there are too many kids." This became their mantra, their excuse from having to interact or participate or remember details about the lives of their grandchildren.

Realize the Potential

Like a stone thrown into a pond, this attitude had rippling ramifications. Their birthday and Christmas gifts to the grandkids—usually the same toy bought in bulk—became tangible reminders of their grandparenting abdication. Their own children felt hurt and alienated. And the grandkids? The grandkids mentally shelved this lack of involvement in the way that most kids do: they accepted it and moved on. No big shakes, that's just the way grandma and grandpa are.

And who were the big losers in this situation? No doubt about it: the grandparents. In living their busy lives, in their travels and church activities and dinners with friends, they made a conscious decision to shut out the grandkids. When the grandchildren were little, this amounted to a free ticket from the burdens and responsibilities of helping to care for small children, but as the children got older the grandparents began to see the ramifications of their earlier default.

The grandchildren went on to develop strong, solid, rewarding ties with their other grandparents, the ones who called and remembered the details of their lives. They called these other grandparents when they had good news, or a rough day at school, or sometimes for no reason at all—just because they "wanted to talk." The girls went shopping with their other grandma, the boys played catch and told jokes and stories with their other grandpa, and the too-busy grandparents were left wondering why no one wanted to hang out with them.

The lesson these grandparents learned the hard way is that while conscious grandparenting can include a lot of hard work, the payback can be tremendous. Quite simply, there is nothing quite as rewarding as a heartfelt hug and kiss from a grateful grandchild who loves you with all their

Chapter One

heart and who knows how much you love them in return. The grandparent/grandchild relationship that can evolve has a potential depth that is unlike any other relationship. And so, a cautionary word of warning: Like anything else in life, if you give up the responsibilities, you'll give up the rewards as well.

Scheduling Time to Grandparent

Some grandparents who lead busy, active lives find it useful to literally schedule time for their grandkids. One grandmother of five makes it a point to call one of her grandchildren each week, "just to chat." She rotates the list, so each child gets a special call about once a month. "I block out a nice large chunk of time and make that call, and then I find out what's going on in that child's life, and we catch up."

If you have several grandchildren you may want to consider making a Grandparent's Notebook. Buy a three-ring binder and insert tabs, one with each grandchild's name. Use the notebook whenever you call your grandchild; make a note of his or her teacher's name, the names of their friends, the classes they take, the hobbies they enjoy. It would be great if you could remember all these details about each grandchild, but the reality is that keeping up with all that information may be impractical. You can use your notebook as a cheat sheet!

The notebook can be anything you want. As the holidays approach, you can make note of any special toys they may mention. You can add photos, pictures the kids draw, recipes you share, journal notes, and entries from times you spend together. Add pages as the children grow; over time, this becomes not only an invaluable resource to use when you call the kids, but it becomes a priceless record of the years, too.

Realize the Potential

Different Styles of Grandparenting

While there are as many different styles of grandparenting as there are grandparents, there are a few readily identifiable styles that tend to emerge. Very few grandparents will fit neatly into just one category. Most tend to have characteristics from two or more categories, though one style usually dominates.

In addition to various elements of each style being present, you may find that you demonstrate more of one type of grandparenting style with one grandchild and morph into another style with another grandchild. You may tend to be authoritarian with a teenager and nurturing with an infant, for example.

Each type of grandparenting has its benefits and drawbacks. By examining each of the different styles, you can pinpoint your own tendencies and be aware of where you may want to fine-tune your style of interacting.

The Authority Figure

It had to happen. Someone had to step in and bring some order to the chaos that currently reigns among your brood. So you stand up straight and begin barking orders. Or…

Everyone in your family knows exactly where you stand on every issue under the sun, and they don't dare disagree for fear of reprisal, because they know that the look you'll cast across the dining room table will be laden with darts, will be low and angry, will be enough to inspire fear in even the bravest heart. Or…

Off Your Rocker!
The Ultimate Guide for Grandparents

Chapter One

Maybe you're a little more low-key in your approach, but the fact remains that you are the Alpha Male or the Matriarch, the one who rules the proverbial roost, and your position is undeniable and supreme.

First, congratulations on your leadership skills. You have a strong personality, and others naturally seem to defer. Your children and grandchildren likely see you as a source of wisdom and knowledge, and you probably almost always get your way.

If you are a strong Authority Figure, even after your kids have grown and left the nest, chances are good that your children have a remnant vestige of fear. Do the kids "hop to" when you issue orders? Why do they continue to defer? These are questions to ask yourself, keeping in mind that once the fear factor is removed, the relationship that may be unearthed could be truer and more sincere.

What on earth am I talking about? Here's an example: Robert is the patriarch in a family of two sons and a daughter. His grown children live within five miles of the house they grew up in, and all the kids continue to work in the family business. Robert is an active and caring participant in the lives of his kids and grandkids; if there is ever a problem, he is there to step in and solve it.

Robert doesn't think he asks for much, but he does have one or two particular wishes. For example, every year he insists that the entire family drop everything to help celebrate his birthday. He wants the whole family there at 6:00 p.m., at his house or at an expensive restaurant, and he always foots the bill. Every year, like clockwork, the whole family gathers and the party begins.

What's the matter with this, you ask? It's Robert's family, Robert is paying the bills, and Robert can do whatever he darn well pleases. Well, yes, to a degree. But...

Realize the Potential

But Robert, whether he's doing it consciously or not, is railroading his family into doing things his way; and even though the proceedings are embellished with lavish meals and generosity, there is still an undeniable element of coercion, which is bound to lead to resentment. And resentment is not good.

What to do, what to do, if you are the Alpha Male or the Matriarch? Learning to back off a bit from your progeny is not an easy thing to do. You love them all dearly and only want what's best for them. But chances are that what you want is inextricably linked with what you *perceive* is "best for them." What if what is truly "best for them" is for them to move 1,500 miles away and start living life on their own terms? Could you bear it?

Some serious soul-searching is in order for most Alpha Males and Matriarchs who truly want a deeper, more satisfying relationship with their kids and grandkids. Beneath the frantic organizing and scheduling of most Type A's lies a fear that things won't be the way they want them to be if they give up the reins.

This is true. But what is also true, once those reins are released, is that you'll find that your kids and grandkids come back whether you're holding the reins or not. Maybe they won't be there for your birthday dinner at 6:00 p.m. sharp, but they'll be there, on their own timetable, when it's best for them, and they will love and appreciate you for giving them the freedom and space to live life on their own terms.

The Party Waiting to Happen

No doubt about it: being a grandparent can be a hoot! Life with grandkids can be a nonstop party, an orgy of sugar and television and staying up until the wee hours, a complete and total absence of regular household rules and schedules. Those lucky kids!

Chapter One

But wait. Having fun with the grandkids doesn't have to entail unmitigated chaos. There may be a better way.

If you find yourself leaning towards "A Party Waiting to Happen" style of grandparenting, you may want to examine your motives for such a relaxed style, and consider the long-term ramifications of such indulgence.

Most children who are lavished with their every heart's desire don't do well in the long run. They become demanding and expectant and, well, spoiled. This is not a matter of finances and how much stuff you are able to afford or provide or lavish on your grandkids; rather, it's a matter of boundaries and setting expectations. An angelic grandbaby who is taught at an early age that anything goes at grandma's may not be so charming a decade down the road.

You may want to rein in your "anything goes" tendencies, though you can still have lots of fun with those grandchildren! No one will think less of you if you impose a few rules in your house. If you don't want kids jumping on the bed, then tell them: "Hey! Kids! No jumping on the bed!" If the kids need to eat something healthy before they gorge on junk, then tell them: "Nothing sweet before dinner!" This is not rocket science, yet many grandparents are reluctant to set boundaries for fear of ruining the party. Don't worry about it. Setting a few boundaries now will save lots of angst in the future. Trust us.

The Nurturer

All grandchildren should be lucky enough to have at least one nurturing grandparent. You've seen them before: these are the grandparents who get down on the floor and play choo-choos, who rock babies to sleep and bake cookies and ply their brood with homemade soup when someone isn't feeling well.

Realize the Potential

These are also the grandparents who tend to lavish their kids or grandkids with attention; to an extent, a nurturer depends on being needed, leaned on, relied upon.

Nurturers give lots of love and affection, but their need for love and affection in return may be a tad bit unrealistic. Most people demonstrate love in the way they would most like to receive love, but if others in the family aren't nurturers as well, then the nurturing grandma or grandpa may feel as though their efforts are not adequately appreciated or rewarded.

If you are a nurturer or have strong nurturing tendencies, you may want to take a step back and evaluate others in your family who may have different styles of interacting. Nurturers display love in a very real, tangible way, and it may be difficult for them to see the affection or love that is shown towards them in less obvious ways.

Kathryn, for example, is a thoughtful, doting grandmother who remembers every birthday and anniversary of those in her sizable family. She sends cards and presents weeks in advance. Kathryn's family members love her and appreciate her thoughtfulness, but tend to take it for granted.

When Kathryn's birthday rolls around, she is hurt enormously if her family members fail to mark the occasion adequately. She wants cards, presents, phone calls… the works. Is Kathryn's desire wrong? Definitely not. Is it unrealistic? Probably.

While Kathryn has the time and inclination to remember dates and events and birthdays and anniversaries, she would do well to keep in mind that a lot of other people just aren't wired that way. It doesn't mean her family doesn't love her; it means they show their love in different ways.

Chapter One

As grandparents, nurturers tend to do best with babies and young children. As grandchildren get older, they usually require less physical coddling, which is one area in particular where nurturing grandparents excel.

One way to bridge this gap is to consciously adapt your way of showing affection to your grandkids. While you may hunk up in bed with a toddler and watch cartoons with him in your lap, you'll have less success with this strategy when your grandson is fourteen!

Instead of smothering your growing grandkids with physical affection, you can adapt your nurturing style and show them affection in ways that they will be more comfortable with. You can help your teenage grandson wash his car, or help your granddaughter braid her hair. As the grandkids get older, your style of showing affection may change, but the love is still there and still strong, and they know it.

The Buffer

"Every generation revolts against its fathers and makes friends with its grandfathers."

—Lewis Mumford

If there's trouble in paradise—conflict between parents, a difficult teenager, financial straits, whatever—a grandparent who acts as a buffer can literally be a family's saving grace.

A buffering grandparent is a communicator and an optimist. He or she may have tendencies to see only the positive side of people and may minimize very real problems or personality flaws in others.

A buffer is generally liked and trusted by other family members. Grandchildren are likely to view a buffering grandparent as an ally, a person who can "reason" with mom and dad, someone who knows them well and is "on their side."

Realize the Potential

One way a buffering grandparent style can come in handy is in the careful navigation of sibling rivalry between grandchildren. A buffer is likely to recognize signs of conflict before any one else even realizes there's a problem, and the buffer can take steps to head off troubles at the pass.

The danger here is in being pulled into family conflicts where you really don't belong. It's great if you can offer counsel and advice to family members in need, but remember what often happens to the messenger: they get shot!

The Sage

Think of Barbara Bush. Billy Graham. Moses. People who have been around the block and learned something along the way.

The sage is the classic grandparent archetype—especially for grandfathers, who often are the keepers of the family's spiritual and religious history and traditions. Known for their wisdom and keen insight, sages are often respected and valued and put up on a pedestal by their families, who cherish the constancy of their values and convictions. When the world around us seems to be falling apart at the seams, there is something wonderfully reassuring about the presence of a sage in our lives.

Family members have a tendency to allow the family sage to see them only at their best. Warts are hidden; no one wants to be thought less of by someone held in such high regard. As a result, the family sage may be presented with a somewhat distorted image of his brood. The only thing he or she sees is the spit-and-polished Sunday best.

True to form, the sage will often see beneath these layers of unintentional deception and will be keenly aware of shortcomings and what is viewed as moral failings in his or her family. This ability to see beneath the layers is what sets a sage apart; there is a wisdom there, a confidence and an ability to say the right thing at exactly the right time.

Off Your Rocker!
The Ultimate Guide for Grandparents

Chapter One

Grandchildren often relate to the sage in the family with love and caution. No one wants to make a mistake in the presence of a sage; children somehow know this intuitively. The challenge, then, if you are a sage, is to let down your guard a bit and let your family see your humanity, flaws and all.

This is much easier said than done. After all, who wants to risk losing the unmitigated love and adoration of a family who sees you as perfect?

But there is an irony here, for the more you risk, the more you gain. Confiding in an older grandchild, for example, about some of the mistakes you made in your life will serve to make you more approachable, more human in his or her eyes.

There are pros and cons to each of the different grandparenting styles we've discussed, but here's the beauty of the system: people change and evolve to suit their circumstances. Just because you tend toward one particular style of grandparenting doesn't mean you can't consciously develop other styles. You may be a fantastic nurturer when your grandchildren are young, for example, then gradually develop into more of a sage. If your teenage grandchildren are headed for trouble, you may be more of an authority figure, with occasional forays into buffer territory. Different approaches are needed at different times, but by being aware of these important roles grandparents can play in the lives of their children and grandchildren, you can best decide which approach will be most useful at any given time.

Relish the Benefits

Though the benefits that grandchildren gain from having close relationships with their grandparents are undeniable, it is also important to remember that grandparents themselves benefit from strong intergenerational relationships as well.

Realize the Potential

How can you benefit from maintaining close ties to your grandchildren? An informal survey of grandparents led to some enlightening answers:

"My grandchildren help keep me young. They encourage me to see things with a younger, fresher perspective. They wear me out, but it's worth it because they challenge me to think new thoughts and physically attempt things that I otherwise probably would not."

"I love to shop with my granddaughter. While I may head towards a stack of solid wool sweaters, she's looking at shiny beaded numbers with feather trim! I love that she includes me in her world. Sometimes it's a lot more fun than mine!"

"I make a real effort to tune in to my grandchildren's world. When they visit, I have them play their music for me (though we usually adjust the volume downwards!), and I watch the TV shows they like to watch, and we occasionally see a movie they want to see. It helps me understand their world, where they're coming from, to take note of the things they find amusing. I show a genuine interest in their world, and they seem to really like the fact that I do."

"Spending time with my grandchildren helps me stay healthy. I don't want to feed them junk, so I eat better when they are around, and we like to go on long walks and bike rides together. Those kids keep me in shape!"

"I am very close to each of my four grandchildren. I call them and we spend as much time together as we can. They enrich my life a great deal. These kids are more than just grandchildren; they are my friends."

So, while building a close relationship with your grandchildren will undoubtedly benefit the kids, it can also be a great source of joy and enrichment in your life, too. The ability to see the world through a child's eyes is a gift that your grandchildren can give you, if you let them.

Off Your Rocker!
The Ultimate Guide for Grandparents

Chapter One

Connecting through the Ages

One grandmother of three takes great joy in seeing the strong family resemblances that run through her brood. "My twelve-year-old granddaughter looks so much like my sister did when she was that age, it just makes me shake my head in wonder. It's like being in a time warp!"

Many grandparents express an appreciation for the fact that their relationships with their grandchildren underscore and strengthen family ties. They feel that the time they spend with their grandchildren is an investment; they can talk to the kids and share stories and memories and lessons that have been passed from generation to generation.

"I love to tell my grandkids stories about when their parents were young! The looks on their faces are priceless when I tell them about the time their father crashed the family Oldsmobile, or about the time when their mother broke her leg falling out of an apple tree."

Noticing, enjoying, and taking pride in the links that connect generations is one of the great pleasures of being a grandparent. Because the younger members of your family have no recollection of the past (they weren't born yet!), they probably lack an appreciation of these familial ties. You are the link!

Before you badger your brood with tales from the past, test the waters first to make sure they are receptive. If you slowly lower yourself into a chair and drone, "I remember the time when your Great Uncle Albert went to the store for some turkey and came back with ham instead...," your grandchildren will likely roll their eyes and go find something else to do. But if you pipe up, "Did you know that your Great Uncle Albert used to be a champion fly fisherman?" you might find yourself with a more receptive audience.

Realize the Potential

Telling stories from the past is a wonderful way to connect through the ages, but photo albums and memorabilia work well, too. Forcing your twelve-year-old granddaughter to sit with you to sift through 300 yellowing photos may not win you many points in the Cool Grandma Department. But if you happen to notice at a certain point that she looks remarkably similar to your sister or your mother when they were her age—and you can show her a photo as proof—then she will more likely be responsive and may even want to see more photos or hear additional stories. And you will be well on your way to connecting through the ages.

The Choice Is Yours

"At the end of your life, you will never regret not having passed one more test, not winning one more verdict or not closing one more deal. You will regret time not spent with a husband, a friend, a child, or a parent."

—Barbara Bush

It is the wise grandparent indeed who realizes and understands the unique relationship that is possible between grandparents and grandchildren. With each grandchild, you have the opportunity to dramatically impact a life, someone to whom you can impart the knowledge you have gleaned and the lessons you have learned, someone who doesn't care about how much money or how many wrinkles you have earned.

Stand in awe of the power you wield as an older, hopefully wiser, and potentially important part of your grandchildren's lives. Your involvement in their lives can mean little—or it can mean a great deal. The choice is yours.

Off Your Rocker!
The Ultimate Guide for Grandparents

Chapter One

Grandma Sunderland

"Our family tells stories when we gather, and when we're in the kitchen cooking we often tell stories about Grandma Sunderland. Remember Grandma's high biscuits? Remember her fried chicken? We describe the flavors, the smells, how her hands looked rolling out sugar cookies. I've joined in the storytelling, but I certainly didn't anticipate becoming 'Grandma Sunderland.' After all, becoming who we are is a little like blindly walking a winding path through the woods, searching for a space between trees. Sometimes it's hard to see clearly.

"Like many modern women, I returned to my family name when I divorced. It seemed a reasonable thing to do and I was deep in the woods, not thinking about the future. Years later, after the requisite twists and turns of living, I finally became a grandmother. I also became a good cook along the way.

"Grandma was a great cook. Her white cookie jar with the red band around the lid was always full of sugar cookies—cookies my sister and I have re-created over the years, some batches more successful than others. Grandma Sunderland made perfect pies; high, rounded loaves of melt-in-your-mouth bread; and the most unforgettable, flaky biscuits. Entering Grandma's kitchen on a cold winter day was like wrapping up in a cozy down comforter filled with fresh bread smells and love.

"I learned to make really fine pies, but perfecting biscuits is an art I keep practicing. Perhaps I'm chasing a myth with my memory, but I remember Grandma's biscuits as high and golden. And, like Jason's Golden Fleece, the reality is just beyond my reach.

"Grandma was a taciturn woman, a farm woman who always wore cotton print dresses with a full apron over the top. She was never too busy to give one of us a hug when we needed it, and she carried little round, hard candies in her pocket as a magic elixir to dry tears. She had white hair all the time I knew her, and it waved back from her face to a neat braid, coiled against the back of her head. Sometimes, if we were lucky enough to stay overnight, we could brush her hair when she took it down.

"The realization that I'd become a second-generation 'Grandma Sunderland' blossomed during a visit with my sister, Judy. She also has a big kitchen, and it's always warm and invit-

Realize the Potential

ing. On this latest trip, her daughter was also visiting, and while we didn't come close to making up a quorum, we were a family gathering. My sister, my niece, and I would cook and tell stories and when I wasn't in the kitchen, I was out in the backyard helping my brother-in-law build a wooden gate and telling more stories.

"One evening, as we began preparations for dinner, I decided to make biscuits. Judy chopped vegetables for a salad as I cut shortening into flour and added enough cold milk to make the dough hold together. Our talk turned to family matters: siblings, children, and the newest member of the family, my new grandson. After cutting out the biscuits and putting them in the hot oven, I showed Judy pictures of this happy grandbaby and bragged about his beauty and charm. Here I was, I laughed, still traipsing around the world like a gypsy looking for a cave, and now I'm a grandmother, too.

"I pulled a nicely browned batch of biscuits from the oven. I couldn't help but lament the fact that while they looked all right, they sure didn't have the height of Grandma Sunderland's majestic creations. My sister's knife stalled in a downward slice through red onion. She turned her head to look at me, a slight frown of puzzlement between her eyes.

"'You're Grandma Sunderland,' she said.

"The realization poured over me as we stared at each other.

"'So I am,' I slowly said.

"We started laughing. We laughed until there were tears rolling down both of our faces. Just then, my niece walked into the kitchen to see what was going on.

"'I'm my own Grandma,' I hooted. When Judy and I settled ourselves enough to talk, we tried to explain why we were laughing, but retelling the story didn't have the same impact.

"The impact, however, has stayed with me. I roll the words around on my tongue, tasting the flavor, absorbing the flesh and fullness of it. What I know about being a grandmother, I learned from her.

"'Grandma Sunderland,' I tell myself. 'I am Grandma Sunderland.' It's a title I wear with pride."

—Contributed by Janet Sunderland

Chapter Two

Making the Connection

"Since you get more joy out of giving joy to others, you should put a good deal of thought into the happiness that you are able to give."

—Eleanor Roosevelt

While a special bond naturally seems to occur between most grandchildren and their grandparents, keep in mind that this is a living, breathing relationship and, like any other, it needs regular amounts of care and attention if it is to thrive. In the words of Dr. Joyce Brothers, "Strong families don't just happen."

A key to building this relationship is an awareness that it must be a two-way street. Not only is it vital for you to impart your knowledge and wisdom to your grandchildren, but it is equally imperative that you take the time to get to know them as individuals, to stop what you are doing long enough to have regular two-way conversations.

A common complaint among school-aged grandchildren is that their grandparents "treat them all the same," "preach too much," or "aren't very good listeners." The good news is that this state of affairs has an easy fix: when you have the opportunity to spend time with your grandchild, make an effort to view the visit as you would the chance to spend time with a friend.

This may be easier said than done, especially if your grandchild is very young. But the point here is to slow down and consider each child as an individual, with individual likes and dislikes, preferences and tastes. Listen to what they want and need, to what their desires are, to what they value and hold dear. Then you will be able to connect to them in an intimate, personal way, and you will be well on your way to establishing a thriving connection with your grandchild.

Making the Connection

The Example of William and Nonny

When Shelly A. was a child, her grandfather, whom she and her cousins were instructed to call "William," was gruff and distant. "One summer William decided that we needed a tree house," says Shelly. "He planned to build the structure in a solitary tree about fifty yards from the house—a country house where the family would often congregate on the weekends. William went to the lumberyard, got the supplies he needed, and fought 100-degree north Texas temperatures and fire ants to build us a stark, lonely fortress. The interior of the tree house felt like a prison; we felt we had been exiled.

"We ventured into the tree house a time or two but soon abandoned it to the fire ants." The perfectly squared corners and watertight roof were left to rot in the elements, a symbol of William's failure to connect. Despite her grandfather's determined efforts, the structure had no soul. "We hadn't been consulted or invited to participate. We weren't the least bit interested."

Shelly's grandmother, on the other hand, whom she and her cousins affectionately called "Nonny," seemed to have no trouble at all connecting with her brood. She'd sit out on the porch with them, cranking ice cream while the kids shot BB guns at tin cans or threw rocks toward the stream. Nonny taught Shelly to whip potatoes and make perfect gravy and sew. "She'd take me to the fabric store on hot summer days and we'd browse among the cool, pungent racks of freshly dyed fabric and fantastically beaded trims."

Nonny had a corner cabinet in her kitchen filled with goodies and sweets, and a shelf she kept stocked with pens, paper, tape, and glue, should her visiting grandkids be inclined to create. She let the kids scarf her weight-loss "chocolates" and "work out" on her exercise machines. "In

Chapter Two

hindsight," Shelly says, "I suppose Nonny was indulgent, but when we visited her we didn't feel spoiled. We simply felt accepted to be ourselves, as long as we behaved, were polite, and were careful not to break or damage anything."

Nonny and William had vastly different approaches to grandparenting: one was cool and aloof, and the other was warm and engaging. "As a child I was careful around William, slightly fearful, not knowing what to expect, but being around Nonny was a balm."

But William kept trying. "William went on to build a mammoth swing set," Shelly continues. "It was so high, you could barely get the swings to sway three feet off the ground. When we got older, he bought the grandkids a horse, built a swimming pool, and helped with college expenses. But we soon learned and felt the vast difference in having a relationship with a grandparent and merely having access to their bank account. Even when William was hard at work building a tree house or a swing set, it felt to us as though we were one more thing on his to-do list. Once he was finished, he crossed it off the list and was done with it."

A very important lesson can be gleaned from the different grandparenting styles of Nonny and William. Kids want you, not your stuff. They don't care if you have a pot of money or build them a fort that reaches to the moon: most kids would rather you sit with them while they play with Barbies or Legos, have a tea party with them, or take them on a bike ride. As with any other relationship, sharing time and experiences is the key to connecting.

Making the Connection

Okay then, how are you to go about connecting with your grandkids? The possibilities are endless, but here are a few ideas:

- **Share a passion.** Find something you like to do and then modify it to an age-appropriate level for your grandkids. If you love to sew, prepare a small sewing kit for your grandchild so you can work on sewing projects together. You can make a small quilt together, or embroider a tablecloth for a granddaughter's dolls. If you love to fish or go bowling or shop 'til you drop, take your grandchild along for the ride. Just be sure to include them and watch them carefully for signs of disinterest or boredom. There can be a fine line between sharing an interest and torturing a small child with something you enjoy that they find interminable!

- **Bend the rules (a little).** When Emma was young, she remembers visiting her grandmother, Nana, who loved to stay up late and watch Johnny Carson. "When I'd visit her we'd prop up in her bed on stacks of pillows and eat ice cream and watch Johnny Carson until the wee hours. I loved that she included me in her little ritual, and to this day I still love to stay up late!"

- **Share your occupation.** Builders or woodworkers, for example, might create a small space in their workroom for grandkids to work with wood right along with them. They could build a birdhouse or a ramp for toy trucks.

- **Learn something new together.** Take your grandchild to the library and learn about something new. Study up on frogs, spaceships, or porcupines. Find out about George Washington's teeth, what makes Jell-O gel, why dandelions grow in the sidewalk,

Chapter Two

what ducks are doing when they dive upside down, what makes the sky blue, or whether or not fish sleep. You can spark your grandchild's imagination with a few well-spent hours in the library and expand your own knowledge base as well.

- **Pass on your values.** No, we're not encouraging you to Hold Forth on Great Themes until your grandchild passes out from boredom; instead, pick a value and then develop a lesson on that theme. For example, let's say you're going to spend the day with your grandchild. On this day, you'd like to share a few thoughts about the importance of being honest. You can communicate this value without beating your grandchild over the head with it. In fact, the more subtle the lesson, the better. You may want to find a book or tell a story that includes as a theme the importance of being honest (*The Boy Who Cried "Wolf!"* would be a good place to start). Then you may want to settle in on the sofa for an afternoon rest and pop in a video. Find a video ahead of time that reinforces the theme of honesty (*Willy Wonka and the Chocolate Factory* would work, or *Annie*: "The one thing you taught me, Miss Hannigan, was 'never tell a lie'!"). Later on that day, you can share a story or two about times when it was difficult for you to tell the truth but why the end result made the effort worth it. You get the picture. Consider the age-old advice to "Show, Don't Tell." And remember that a dialogue on any subject will always be more effective than a monologue.

Making the Connection

- **Explore the interests your grandchild has.** If your grandson is really into ice hockey, you can arrange to take him to a game, take him skating, or read up on the sport together while you "surf the net." A grandchild who is showing an interest in space would be thrilled with a trip to the planetarium, or an evening spent stargazing in a big, open field.

- **Pay attention to special toys or interests.** Your grandchild's interests are likely to include one or more characters that in some way derive from a slick retail operation. Items such as Pokémon trading cards, American Girl dolls and accessories, Polly Pockets (teensy little plastic dolls and accessories), Teletubbies, or characters from Sesame Street all may capture your grandchild's imagination at one time or another. You'll win big points if you ride these waves when they occur, but this doesn't have to cost a fortune (though it very well could if you let it). Many of the popular retail characters are featured in movies that you can buy or rent. If your grandchild loves a certain type of doll, you can focus on that particular doll without buying a thing. For example, you can arrange to have a tea party with American Girl dolls, or set up a play area in an out-of-the-way area for Polly Pockets or Barbies or Matchbox cars or whatever it is that your grandchild loves playing with the most. Keep in mind that these interests can change quickly; if it's been a while since you've seen your grandchildren, you'll want to check with them or their parents to make sure the toy de jour hasn't changed.

Chapter Two

- **Keep some toys on hand.** You'll win big points if you occasionally cruise by garage sales and make it a point to periodically update your toy box (every self-respecting grandparent has one!). Get a big plastic bin at Target (they usually sell for about five dollars) and fill it with age-appropriate toys for when your grandkids come to visit. But more about that later.

- **Meet your grandchild's friends.** If at all possible, make an effort to get acquainted with your grandchildren's best friends. When you visit your grandchildren in their home, encourage them to have some friends come over to play, then spend some time interacting with them and getting to know them a bit. Be careful not to overdo it; you don't want to be a source of embarrassment! But getting to know your grandchildren's friends gives you one more common point of reference, one more thing about them that you can inquire about knowledgeably, one more way for you to communicate to them that you want to know about them and what goes on in their lives.

- **Introduce your grandchildren to your friends.** Arrange to have afternoon tea with a friend or two, and include your grandchild in the party. "This is my friend Sue, who loves to dance, and this is my friend Carol, who makes gingerbread houses every year at Christmas...." Be careful not to let the conversation veer too far from what your grandchild will know or care about. This is an opportunity to share your life and your friends with your grandchild, one more way to weave the strands of your lives together. An added bonus: showing off your grandchild in front of your friends is a great way to

Making the Connection

make your grandchild feel special. This can be a great way to boost his or her self-esteem.

- **Spend time together.** Spend as much time as you can alone with your grandchildren, without their parents hovering nearby. Once the grandkids get a little bit older, you might even consider taking a trip with them. Overnight camping trips are a great way to cram a lot of quality visiting into a relatively short period of time, and camping provides the additional benefit of an environment that is free of computers and television. And be sure to turn off those cell phones!

- **Give each of your grandchildren a special nickname.** The names can be silly or sentimental. "Pumpkin Pie," "Scrap Iron," "Button Nose," "Little Bit," "Cuddle Bug"… the name itself doesn't matter, but nicknames are intimate and personal and are a great way to help forge a bond with your grandchildren.

- **Develop private rituals together.** One grandfather always makes it a point to bake biscuits with his granddaughter when they see each other. One grandmother always offers Wrigley's spearmint gum every time she sees her grandson. One grandfather has developed a secret handshake with each of his grandchildren. One grandmother has a special candle she lights whenever her grandchild comes to visit. Look for ways to turn the ordinary into a special occasion.

- **Resist the urge to over-schedule.** While you may want to make some special plans when you know you'll have the grandkids for a day, a weekend, or a week, be sure to build some down time into your schedule, too. Keep an occasional morning or after-

Chapter Two

noon free of planned activities and just see what pastimes naturally evolve. You may find yourself cuddling in bed with a little one at 11:00 a.m. or baking cookies at lunchtime. In many cases, the most special times you'll have with your grandchildren don't occur when you're busy working your way down a preplanned schedule, but instead when you are both relaxed and unhurried.

- **Finally, when you spend time with your grandchildren, live in the moment.** Forget the piles of laundry, the chores that need to be done, and turn off *Oprah*. Consciously bring yourself into the moment, and pay attention to the details. Notice the softness of your grandchild's cheek, the curl in her hair, the lilt in her voice. Pay attention to and savor these fine details, for it is in noticing and appreciating these snapshots of fleeting childhood that you'll discover the magic.

Conversation Starters

"A long time ago I learned a secret. I learned that everybody is hurting a little bit somewhere. I have to keep telling myself to remember this. No matter what they ask, most folks don't really want to know about me. They want me to know about them."

—from *Then God Created Grandparents
and It Was Very Good* by Charlie Shedd

As with any other type of meaningful relationship, connecting with grandchildren starts with conversation. If you want to get to the heart and soul of a person—even a little person—you're going to have to get beyond the niceties and talk about something besides the weather.

Making the Connection

There are differences, however, between communicating with children and communicating with adults. Most adults are skilled, at least to a functional degree, at basic conversations. And while some kids are natural-born chatterboxes (one grandmother used to say to her talkative granddaughter, "You could talk a dog off a meat wagon!"), some are not and will need a little bit of help in becoming verbally proficient.

Children tend to be very perceptive. They sense when you want to spend time with them and when you'd rather focus on other things. Much of their communication is nonverbal, too. A grandchild may plop down in your lap or give you a spontaneous, sloppy kiss—nonverbal ways of communicating, to be sure.

Once you begin developing relationships with each of your grandchildren, you will begin to notice subtle differences in the way they communicate. A loquacious eight-year-old may talk your ear off, while his two-year-old sister says all she has to say with a grunt and a friendly smack on the leg with her toy bunny.

Pay attention to what the kids say and what they try to communicate via other means. We will examine some of the differences between kids of different ages in more depth in the next chapter, but here are a few communications pointers:

Baby Talk

Talking to infants can seem like a lost cause… if you're not paying attention. If you are, though, you will immediately see that your words are listened to and studied intently. Babies love to be talked to, though their verbal appreciation extends to other types of sounds as well. Babies love it when you gurgle, cluck, whistle, and sing. Most tend to gravitate toward low, soothing voices. If your voice tends to be high-pitched, make a conscious effort to speak softly around very young children and infants.

Chapter Two

Okay, so you should talk to your infant grandchildren. About what? Here you're off the hook: it doesn't really matter what you talk about, so long as you're talking. You can tell your infant grandchild about the weather, about what you're going to prepare for dinner, about how silly his parents are, about how beautiful his mother was at her wedding. You can talk about your friends, your poodle, or Elvis. And here's another benefit to all this talking: while you yammer on, your grandchild is memorizing the sound of your voice, mentally shelving it, so the next time he sees you and hears your voice it will help him recognize you. You're laying a foundation now for a deeper relationship later on, and it's never too soon to start.

Toddler Talk

Talking to toddlers can be frustrating, but it can also be a lot of fun. For very young children, sometimes the most successful conversations are the simplest. You can talk about colors ("What color is the sky? Is that your favorite color?"). Ask children who are just learning to talk questions that you already know the answers to ("What is your sister's name? What is your puppy dog's name?"). You'll give them an opportunity to use words they know, and you'll help build confidence in their ability to communicate.

If it's been a long time since you've spent time with toddlers, here's a word of caution about talking around little ones: Watch what you say! Children this age are busy memorizing everything they hear. The one thing you say around your grandchild that you would least like to hear repeated back to their parents is the one thing he or she will run home and report. Guaranteed!

Making the Connection

Older Kids

Once your grandchildren are past the toddler stage, communication really has the potential to take off. Now, phone conversations become much more feasible, practical and understandable. You can ask questions and have them answered in a meaningful way.

For older kids, ask lots of questions, and be sure to tell your grandkids details about your life, too. Ask your six-year-old grandson about his best friend, then tell him about yours. Another way to pave the path for smooth communication: don't force it. Children will tell you what's on their minds if you spend some unhurried time with them and let the conversation naturally unfold.

Older kids love to hear stories, which helps them understand their family history and reinforces their tribal sense of belonging. Stories don't have to be lengthy or involved: try to focus on the high points and fill in the details if your grandchild shows interest and begins to ask questions. You can tell your grandson about his crazy great-grandfather who once rode a horse from Austin to Houston to ask a girl out on a date ("and *she* later became your great-grandmother!"); you can tell your granddaughter that the quilt she loves to snuggle under while watching TV was made by her sweet Aunt Ruth, who baked pies every weekend to take to the local nursing home. The stories themselves don't matter (though it helps to keep them positive), but the family connection is vitally important.

Finally, communication with older kids need not be limited to conversations. Mail and e-mail can also be used very effectively at this age.

Chapter Two

Teens: Learning the Lingo

Communicating with teenagers tends to go one of two ways: you may have a gregarious teenage grandchild who talks nonstop, or you may find yourself with a quiet, brooding teen who doesn't communicate much at all.

If you have a talkative teen in the family, then chances are you need no help in eliciting thoughts, comments, or suggestions, but you may want a few pointers for the quieter ones. Here we go:

In many cases a quiet teen is a confused, self-conscious teen in disguise. Chances are that what your teenage grandchild needs from you is a quiet, reassuring presence. You don't have to talk all the time; just spending time together may be of tremendous meaning and significance to your grandchild.

When you spend time with a quiet teenage grandchild, resist the urge to ask lots of detailed, probing questions. Asking, "So, do you have a girlfriend?" will probably get you nowhere with a recalcitrant teen. However, "Tell me what's going on with you these days," may open up a door. The key here is to avoid, at all costs, the perception of judgment. It's not your job to judge your grandchildren—thankfully, that's their parents' job. You're off the hook. You are free to just hang out with your grandchildren and be their friend.

Here's a great idea: If you have preteen or teenage grandchildren, make it a point to occasionally buy and read magazines that are devoted to teens. Pay attention to who's hot, what the kids are wearing, and the words and phrases they use. By observing the world in which they live, you will begin to grasp some of the subtle nuances of the teenage subculture, and you will start to close some of the distance between the generations, as your grandkids perceive that you aren't the old fuddy-duddy they imagined.

Making the Connection

This isn't to say that you need to emulate what you read about in teen magazines, by the way! But a passing awareness of who's in, who's out, and why will communicate to your grandkids that you care about what is important to them.

Sharing Faith and Spiritual Values

"My grandmother makes me think that God is her best friend."

—from *Then God Created Grandparents and It Was Very Good* by Charlie Shedd

As the children get older, you may find yourself sharing stories of more depth and significance. You may have a strong faith or religious beliefs and want to share those with your grandchildren.

If your own children have very different beliefs from you, you'll need to tread softly in this area. The parents won't be one bit appreciative if their children come back from visits with you in a state of religious confusion, sporting Rastafarian dreadlocks and spouting existential angst. Watch out if you convert a grandchild to a faith his parents don't share—future visits might come to a screeching halt.

But you can share your faith just as you would share any other facet of your personality. If you love doing jigsaw puzzles, for example, then your grandchildren will naturally know this about you and will learn about puzzles from you. As with other aspects of your personality, your beliefs and your faith can and should be shared if they are important to you.

One of the best ways to share deeply held beliefs is to read books together and tell stories. You can tell your grandchild about how your faith helps you. But keep in mind that lessons of faith should always be gentle and reassuring.

Chapter Two

"Simply to be in my granny's presence, content and without tension, was sufficient demonstration of love. Her spirituality shone like a lamp from within. When she moved from a room, it was as if the flames of the fire had grown smaller, or the light had been lowered."

—Molly Parkin, from *Moll: The Making of Molly Parkin*

While you are discussing deep personal matters of faith and conviction, you can share other important life lessons as well.

"My grandfather was a repeated failure in business, but he always told me that his real regret in life wasn't that he didn't make a million bucks, but that he didn't spend enough time with his family," says one young father of two. "I think about that when I'm putting in too much time at the office. I don't want to make that same mistake and have that same regret when I'm older."

Success is in the Details

Cards, letters, small gifts, and phone calls…these are all great ways to let your grandkids know you're thinking of them. We'll look at more specific ways to connect in Chapter 5 (Long-Distance Grandparenting), but in the meantime keep in mind that it is the small things that count most. One whopping-big Christmas or birthday gift doesn't register nearly as much on the Grandchild Richter Scale as five or six unexpected, small gifts given throughout the year. Remember, it's not your stuff that grandkids want most. It's you.

One grandmother, Lynn C., has a small shelf in her closet set aside for items for her grandkids, who range in age from three to thirteen. The shelf contains things like perfume and makeup samples, shampoo bottles from hotels she's visited, pens, and little balls—freebies from trade shows she attends through work. For her younger grandkids, Lynn has a great idea: Whenever she stops by an occasional fast food restaurant to grab a quick lunch, she always orders a kid's meal, then saves the toy.

Making the Connection

None of the items on her grandchild shelf cost much: in fact, most of them were free. But when the grandkids come to visit, there's always a small pile of gifts for each of them, and that small pile conveys more to the kids than a mile-high stack of Christmas presents ever could: it says, loud and clear, that Lynn has been thinking of them, not just on one shopping trip, but frequently and consistently.

If you make it a habit to pick up small gifts throughout the year, take a half-hour now and then and mail a few off to the kids (even if they live nearby). A small package of stickers, book marks, and photos, for example, will thrill your grandchildren and reinforce the bond between you.

One really great way to reinforce the special times you've had together is to share pictures and build photo albums together. Make it a point to take lots of photos when you spend time with your grandchildren. (A word about vanity: don't let wrinkles or gray hair keep you from allowing your grandchildren to have a permanent record of your special times together.) A blank photo album can be a great gift to a grandchild: keep it at your house and the two of you can add to it together whenever your grandchild comes to visit. If you have several grandchildren, let them each have their own book.

One clever grandfather who is handy with a video camera keeps separate videos for and of each grandchild. When the kids come to visit he pops in the different video tapes and records special clips for each grandchild on their very own tape. There may be only a few moments from each session, but watching the single tape is a brief journey through childhood and shared moments together. The grandkids love those tapes!

Chapter Two

Cultivating Rituals

One way to connect with your grandchildren is to develop shared rituals. These rituals can be simple or elaborate. As you discover the likes and preferences of each grandchild, you can build on those to develop a few pastimes that the two of you enjoy doing together.

For example, one grandmother has discovered that one of her grandsons really loves playing with and is fascinated by bugs. This grandmother loves to garden. So she helped her grandson build a bug house, a small, portable container that lets him capture and keep bugs, and when he comes to visit the two of them head outdoors, where grandma gardens and her grandson happily catches bugs beside her.

One grandfather, an early riser, wakes his oldest granddaughter when she is visiting and they go get breakfast together—just the two of them.

One active grandmother takes her teenage granddaughter with her to the health club, where they work out together when her granddaughter comes to visit.

Make a conscious effort to discover and nurture the unique aspects of your relationship with each grandchild. The rituals that you develop together will help cement your bond well past the age of childhood.

Making the Connection

Respect the Uniqueness of Each Grandchild

As you spend time with your grandchildren, don't expect to feel exactly the same way about each child, and don't expect to have identical relationships with all of them. Susan Kettmann, M.S.Ed., author of *The 12 Rules of Grandparenting*, says this: "Unfortunately, when grandparents strive to love each grandchild with absolute equality, the results can be bland and mediocre. It is entirely possible that loving equally is the easy way out."

Children are just as individualistic as adults, and your personal chemistry will vary from child to child. You may have some grandchildren that you have a lot in common with, and some with whom you really have to work to find some common ground. While those grandchildren who you naturally bond with can provide solid, meaningful, rewarding relationships, those you have to work on can also be very rewarding.

Don't give up on the more challenging grandchildren. Look for ways to connect. Take them shopping or to a bookstore and observe the things they are drawn to. Ask questions. Tell stories. Spend time with them. In many cases, the very kids that are more challenging are the ones who need you the most.

Chapter Two

Remember What Is Important

It can be difficult to have small children around when you haven't had them underfoot for years. Accidents can and do happen. Messes get made, things get broken, dirt gets tracked in, and toys get strewn. You and your grandchildren will have a much more enjoyable time together if you can resign yourself to these inevitabilities and just relax.

When Rachel was seven, she remembers turning a corner in her grandmother's house and accidentally bumping into a table where her grandmother's prized porcelain nativity was set up for Christmas. "It was one of those slow-motion moments where I realized what I had done and turned to see one of the tall porcelain figures rocking back and forth. I reached out to try to stop its fall, but it was too late. The Wise Man fell to the floor and shattered.

"I stood there, too stunned to speak, and then I began to cry. My grandmother rushed to see what all the commotion was about, gently moved me away from the broken glass, then said such sweet, kind words that I remember them still.

"'Oh, Rachel, don't worry about a silly old knick knack. Look, only the base broke off. I'm sure it can be fixed! In the meantime we'll just make him the sleeping Wise Man!'"

"Then she laid the Wise Man on his side and pulled me into her lap and told me that I was much more important to her than any old holiday decoration. Later that day, when I looked at the nativity set, the broken Wise Man was gone. It was like she took him away so I wouldn't even have to be reminded of my blunder.

"I know she loved that nativity set," says Rachel. "But in that moment, she conveyed to me instantly and unreservedly how much more I meant to her and how much she loved me."

How much more valuable did that nativity set become, now short a Wise Man, once it became a tool to convey to a child how much she was loved and cherished?

Making the Connection

Tulips

Growing up, I was one of the luckiest girls I knew. Not only were my grandparents living, but they lived very close by. I got to spend a lot of time at their home. There were even nights that I got to spend the night and catch the school bus from their house the next day.

These were special times for me. I can remember that spring was an extra special time. Each spring, when the trees budded and the flowers began to bloom, there was one flower in particular that I would wait for. It was a red and white tulip. My grandma's only tulip. This flower grew in the shade of the front row of trees at her house. Grandma said she didn't know how it got there; she hadn't planted it. But every year it grew. No fertilizer, no extra water, no extra care, not much sunlight, but year after year it grew, and Grandma and I thought it was beautiful.

One year I wasn't doing very well in school and I was sure that my teacher didn't like me very much, but I came up with a plan to change that. That winter, months before the tulip would bloom, I went to my grandma and asked her if I could give that flower to my teacher. Grandma didn't ask why. She didn't say "but that's our special flower." She just said "yes."

I was so excited. I didn't think that winter would ever end. I waited and waited. Finally the trees got their buds and the flowers started to bloom and that tulip came up. That morning before the bus came I ran into the house. "Grandma, the tulip is coming up! Can I have it now?" For a moment I was afraid that she had forgotten. But she hadn't. She went to the front window and looked out. "Not yet, honey, it's not ready yet."

This scenario went on for what seemed like forever. I was beginning to think that Grandma was going to go back on her promise. I was afraid that when that tulip actually bloomed she would remember how beautiful it was and decide that she wanted to keep it. I should have known better... this was my Grandma. About the time that I had given up hope of ever getting that tulip

Chapter Two

and remedying the strained relations I had with my teacher, Grandma came and found me while I was getting ready for school. She had a pair of scissors, a wet paper towel and a piece of aluminum foil in her hands. She looked at me with a loving smile on her face. "Honey, it's ready now." I ran out the front door and happily harvested the tulip. She helped me wrap the wet paper towel around the stem and carefully place the foil around the paper towel.

I remember how wonderful I felt as I left for school that day. I remember everything about that morning like it was yesterday. Everything up until the time I got on the bus. I have no memory of giving that special flower to my teacher. I have no idea if she liked it or if she liked me more because of it. That wasn't the important part.

For several years in the spring, Grandma let me take that beautiful red and white tulip to school to give to one of my teachers. I never remember the teachers' response, but I will never forget the love in her eyes as she helped me wrap it up to take it to school.

That has been many years ago now, but my favorite flower is still a red and white tulip. I have about fifty tulips in all different colors that bloom in front of my house every year, and every year my two daughters come to me and ask if they can pick one to take to their teachers. I am ashamed to admit that up until last year my response has always been no. I love my tulips. I enjoy every minute of watching them bloom. It is my favorite time of the year. It wasn't until my grandma passed away last year that I realized how special it made me feel that she would give me her only tulip. I silently made a promise to her that every year I would help my girls pick out the two most beautiful tulips from my flower garden to take to their teachers. I want them to know that they are even more precious to me than my prized tulips.

—Contributed by Mary Jo Brooks

Chapter Three

Breaking It Down By Age

Just how ambitious was Grandma Jones when it came to her grandchildren? Well, when a stranger inquired as to their ages, she replied, "The doctor's in the third grade and the rocket scientist is in the fifth."

—Anonymous (from *Grandmothers* by Helen Exley)

If it's been awhile since you've had kids under your roof, they may seem to you to be alien creatures. Have kids really changed that much?

Well, yes and no. There are probably some very real, tangible differences in the way you were raised, the way you raised your kids, and the way your grandchildren are being raised. Change happens.

The changes may be subtle or obvious. Maybe you grew up in an idyllic household where dad brought home the bacon, kissed mom on the cheek and all was well. Maybe your own marriage didn't do so well and you divorced. And maybe your grandchild is being raised in a single-parent home. Maybe you grew up in a God-fearing Italian Catholic household; maybe your grandchildren are being raised as vegetarian Buddhists. These are dramatically different conditions in which to be raised. Coming to terms with the differences in the way you experienced life and the way your grandchildren are living can be a challenge.

Off Your Rocker!
The Ultimate Guide for Grandparents

Chapter Three

That said, there are also likely to be similarities in what you recall from your own experience and the realities that your grandchildren face. There is a great deal of truth in the old saying, "The more things change, the more they stay the same."

While your grandchildren may have many more toys, clothes, and possessions than you ever dreamed of, they still have a fundamental desire to interact, to communicate, to be held and kissed and loved. The important things don't change.

Remember, too, that connecting with children is an art. As with any other endeavor, the more you practice the better you get. You may initially hold your newborn grandchild with fear and trepidation, thinking to yourself, "What now?" But the more you make yourself available to that child, physically and emotionally, the more confident and comfortable you will become.

Infants

The key to interacting with infants is to make a primal connection. This does not mean you have to mark the infant with obscure tribal symbols or guard the hut with a sharpened spear. What it does mean, however, is that you need to be aware of the level at which the child is interacting and bonding. For infants, scent, sound, and eye contact are the primary ways they relate to those around them.

Translation, please? Okay, let's say your newborn grandchild has arrived. You're headed to the hospital, eager to meet the newest member of the family. Now, this may seem like a minor point, but go easy on the smelly stuff. If you douse yourself in perfume, hairspray, deodorant, or scented powder, you are likely to send startling olfactory messages to the baby. Go easy on artificial scents. Deodorant and a small dab of perfume or cologne, if necessary, are all you should use. Much more than that will overwhelm the baby, who may cry or squirm to get away (especially once he is a cou-

Breaking It Down By Age

ple of months old). Also, be consistent with the scents you choose. For example, wear the same perfume or cologne every time you see the baby. This will help the child identify you, along with… (drum roll, please)…

Your voice. Infants are remarkably well attuned to individual voices. At birth, they are able to recognize their mother's and often their father's voices, having heard them while in the womb. You'll want to lower your voice; keep it low and soothing. A high-pitched, shrill, or loud voice is likely to startle the baby, and startled babies usually cry. This is not the effect we're going for here.

Talk to the baby. Introduce yourself. "Hello, sweetheart. It's so nice to finally get to meet you! I'm Grandma Kelly and we are going to have so much fun together…." It doesn't matter what you say, but what is important is that you let the baby hear and get accustomed to your voice. Tell stories, sing songs, or just talk about what you're going to do that day.

Now, while you're busy talking to the baby, be sure to look at the baby, too. Make eye contact. Newborn infants generally are able to focus at about a foot away, so you don't have to hold them too close, but they won't see you if you talk to them from across the room, either. Once you make eye contact, hold it. The baby will study your face, your hair, and your features with great intensity. It's almost as though the baby is trying to memorize your face, and, in a sense, that is exactly what the child is doing.

Once the infant is about six months old, you may want to try "the Nanny Trick." (Judy has honed this brilliant maneuver to a fine art form.) Quite simply, invest in a few high-quality, long necklaces that have shimmery, shiny, jangly things attached. Buy the pieces carefully—you want to make sure there is nothing that could either scratch the infant or break off and pose a choking hazard. You will soon refer to these shiny, jangly necklaces as your "baby mag-

Off Your Rocker!

The Ultimate Guide for Grandparents

Chapter Three

nets," for that is exactly what they are. Once the baby is several months old you will find that the instant the baby sees you, his eyes narrow to slits as he visually searches for his accessory "treat"! (You don't have to be a grandmother to use "the Nanny Trick." It works just as well for men, though they may feel a little bit silly at first wearing chunky costume jewelry!)

For long-distance grandparents, make an effort to let the infant become accustomed to your voice. Make a tape recording of yourself reading a children's classic, such as Goodnight Moon. Have the parents play the tape frequently, especially before your visits. Then, when you are with the child, be sure to read the same book there, in person. Write a letter to your grandchild, which the parents can put in their scrapbook; it will be read and cherished in the years to come.

With infants, though, the key is physical contact. If you are in the same room as the baby, hold it, cuddle it, and carry it around with you as you putter about. Go on walks together. Put the baby in a carrier or stroller and head outside, and as you walk you can point out various sights and sounds. It doesn't matter that the baby won't understand a word you're saying. What is important is that you are spending time with the baby doing things that allow him to register your voice, your smell, and your presence.

On a practical note, if you anticipate having the opportunity to do any babysitting at your house, you may want to consider a few advance preparations. The sky is the limit here. Some grandparents set aside a whole room for the baby—a nursery, where they can keep a crib, changing table, rocking chair, and toys and supplies such as diapers, wipes, pacifiers, teethers, and extra clothes. Others set aside a drawer in the kitchen or a basket in the pantry where they keep their "baby supplies."

Breaking It Down By Age

If you are jumping with joy at the thought of babysitting your infant grandchild, then keeping your own baby supplies on hand will go a long way towards convincing the baby's parents that you are prepared and that you are serious about your offers to help. The fact that you are well-stocked also alleviates some of the burden of shuffling bags of baby stuff to grandma's house, which can be more trouble than it's worth—from the parents' point of view, anyway.

So then, what will you need?

Put a package of diapers and wipes at the top of your list. If it's been years since you last changed a diaper, ask the baby's mother to show you how. You don't need a changing table; any old towel will do. But what you do need to remember, especially as the baby gets a bit older, is to *never* leave the baby unattended on a changing table, bed, or any elevated surface. You'd hate to have to report to the baby's parents that the child rolled over for the first time—off the bed and onto the floor!

Next on the list: feeding supplies. This list will be greatly minimized if the baby is exclusively breastfed, in which case you probably won't be doing much solo babysitting anyway since the mother will be unable to go very far for very long. But, as the baby gets older and less dependent on the breast, you will be able to help feed him or her, so having a few supplies on hand is a good idea. A bib, a few bottles, a small baby spoon, and a few jars of baby food should do the trick.

Finally, having a few changes of clothes—a play outfit or two and a couple of pairs of pajamas, along with extra socks—means that the child will have everything he needs at your house. Your house will become a veritable home away from home. The child will have the necessities, the parents will be oh-so-appreciative, and the task of babysitting will be greatly simplified because you have what you need at hand.

Chapter Three

Toddlers

Love is patient and kind.

—1 Corinthians 13:4

While toddlers are great fun, they also require a great amount of work. If your grandchildren are in the twelve- to thirty-six-month range, get ready for lots of laughs and lots of action.

While we generally advise against smothering grandchildren with tons of toys or gifts, since the last thing you want to do is encourage rampant materialism, it is a good idea to occasionally offer small presents or treats. This communicates to your toddler grandchildren that you care about them and have been thinking about them. Children this age are very literal. They understand "I love you" in vague, general terms, but they have a clearer understanding when you say, "I love you, and here's a Matchbox car in my pocket just for you!"

If you live far away and only see your young grandchildren occasionally, you will want to pay particular attention to the way you greet them. When you first see them, at the airport or at the front door, resist the urge to rush at them and smother them with a loud and frightening approach. Instead, be calm and quiet and gentle. Let them come to you. Offer a small gift, then a gentle hug. Get on their level, even if it means finding a chair at the airport so you can sit and then lean down to make eye contact at their level.

Once they warm to you, which may take a few minutes or several hours, you can begin to interact gently. Have them come sit next to you on the couch, or you can sit down on the floor next to them. Ask them to show you their favorite toys. Once they produce the favored toy, make sure to examine it carefully, to nod in approval, to ooh and ahh and show

Breaking It Down By Age

that you appreciate the particular attributes of this exquisite toy—even if it's a ratty stuffed animal that looks like it's probably a carrier of the plague.

Ask about their playmates. "Who do you like to play with?"

Ask them what they like to do.

Ask them what they like to eat, what they prefer to wear, and what they enjoy watching on TV.

While it is not Twenty Questions, this inquisitive interaction demonstrates to your toddler grandchildren that you care about and are interested in them.

Now, you may not be able to understand what they are saying (this is especially true for telephone conversations, when you will have to decipher their toddler talk without the aid of visual clues). In these instances avoid the natural reaction, "What did you say?" Instead, be liberal with nods and vague rejoinders. "Is that right?" "Really?" "How about that!" Remember that these are not in-depth conversations about serious life issues. You want to reinforce their attempts to communicate, not badger them or frustrate them by their limited verbal abilities.

Keep in mind that toddlers have a very real need to be physically active. It's not that they want to squirm and hop and jump and run... it's that they *need* to squirm and hop and jump and run. You will solve a lot of problems before they even arise if you plan activities that take into account this need to be active. Trips to the park, to the zoo, to the aquarium, or just an hour or two of romping in the back yard will help meet their need to move about and exercise growing muscles and bones.

Because kids this age need to move about, and because they also have an almost insatiable curiosity about the world around them, you may want to make a special effort to keep

Chapter Three

them away from places where danger or damage lurk. Grocery shopping with a toddler can be a challenge, and it's wise to stay way away from stores that display lots of trinkets, knick-knacks, or breakables. Really.

Remember that kids this age are motivated by a powerful desire to learn. Taking a trip to the library together or to a local book store can be a great way to keep them both physically and mentally stimulated. Check your paper to find out if your local library or bookstore is offering a special storytime for kids.

A word here about food, what toddlers eat, what they tend to shun, and what you can reasonably expect from them at the dinner table.

Take your cue from the parents on this one. If the parents have gone to great lengths to keep the child's diet healthy, you will cause great consternation and grief if you cheerfully introduce the child to Frooty Pebbles, strawberry milk, and Cheez Whiz.

On the other hand, if the child generally enjoys a diet filled with processed foods and sugar, you'll have an unpleasant battle on your hands if you insist on an appreciation of brussels sprouts and broccoli.

Talk to the parents before the grandkids come to visit, and talk about the parents' wishes and the child's preferences. Keep a few child-friendly staples on hand at all times, tried-and-true concoctions such as peanut butter and jelly, macaroni and cheese, and chicken nuggets. Have some lemonade mix available, and store a roll of cookie dough in the freezer. You may be able to sneak some kid-friendly vegetables onto the scene; items such as corn, green beans, or peas are usually regarded with something less than full-fledged contempt.

Breaking It Down By Age

The idea here is to offer food the kids will eat, real food that will prevent them from being fueled by junk alone.

Don't be surprised or frustrated when a visiting toddler is inquisitive. You can fully expect the child to want to inspect your hair, face, clothes, cabinets, and drawers. They will look around a room, look at items in the room, then look for items under the sofa or under the rug. When taking walks, they will frequently stop to examine flowers, bugs, or cracks in the sidewalk. Kids this age are slow and methodical. Don't expect to go anywhere or do anything in a hurry. It can take them five minutes to find their coat, locate a favorite toy, put on their shoes, or take a sip of milk. Patience is key when dealing with toddlers. P-a-t-i-e-n-c-e.

If you plan on doing any babysitting in your home, be sure to have a special corner of a centrally located room set aside where you keep a stash of age-appropriate toys and books. (If you put the children's supplies in an out-of-the-way, seldom-used room, they'll feel banished and won't want to go there. Small kids want to be where the action is, and they want to be physically close to you.)

You'll still need a few basic supplies on hand, such as diapers, wipes, pajamas and an extra change of clothes. At this age, food probably won't be as much of an issue. You may want to keep a few bottles on hand—some toddlers use a bottle to help them go to sleep. However, this can corrupt little teeth, so make sure that you only do this (give them a bottle before going to bed or taking a nap) *if that is what their parents want you to do.*

Chapter Three

Young Children (4–8)

With young children, you want to make an effort to hone your listening skills. Children this age are engaged by sharing activities and doing things together. You don't have to make particular plans for spending time with young children (although a special outing or two would likely be greatly appreciated). Instead, teach your grandchildren to do whatever it is you like to do: cook, garden, sew, or go fishing. If the grandkids are staying with you for a week and you need to clean up the house a bit, give them a dust rag and let them help, or teach them to polish silver. It doesn't matter what you do with young grandchildren; what is important is that you do *something*.

Young children are blessedly able to entertain themselves for awhile, which is something you will probably appreciate after having spent much time with them as toddlers! With young children, you can show them how to do something then let them go, free to experiment and discover and be productive on their own. You can give a young girl a small bag of fabric and trim and let her make a purse for her dolls. You can give a young boy a jump rope or basketball and let him play for hours.

Children this age are still motivated by a powerful desire to learn. They are driven to read, explore, and ask questions. Many kids this age seem to want to talk nonstop; the wise grandparent will take advantage of this garrulous tendency and use it to get to know their grandchildren well.

You can take advantage of this desire to learn by telling your young grandchildren lots of stories and showing them family pictures and mementos. Children this age are fascinated by new knowledge of any kind. You can read books together, watch cooking shows on TV, or check out a new ethnic grocery store that just opened nearby. Consider your young grandchildren as adventurers: they'll be open to just about anything.

Breaking It Down By Age

'Tweens (8–12)

This is one of the easiest age groups with which to interact, but also one of the more intimidating. This is the age when children reach outside of themselves and their family structure and begin to seek the approval of peers. It is also a time of intense communication; kids this age need to talk, and they need you to listen. Be prepared for important issues to crop up in conversation; kids this age are more aware of the world around them and are likewise more aware of the issues in their own immediate family. They may need you to help them sort out questions of identity and conflict.

'Tweens may be counted on to find the discrepancies or areas of incongruity between you and their parents. If the parents are particularly religious and you are not, for example, they may have very real, legitimate questions about this state of affairs.

"Why don't you go to church, Grandma?"

You may make it a point to visit a retirement center or regularly contribute to society in some other way. Your grandchild may recognize that these are things his or her parents don't do. How do you explain it?

First, be honest in your answers, but be careful, too. This is dangerous ground. You want to communicate your beliefs without minimizing or belittling the beliefs of others—especially those of the parents. Strive to be nonjudgmental, which will free your grandchildren up to be open and honest in their conversations with you.

If a particularly thorny issue arises, like, "Why did my dad leave us?" or some other disturbing or horrifying question, this is a prime time to sit down with your grandchild and have an honest, heart-to-heart talk. Your grandchild is opening his or her heart and needs a familiar, comforting person to provide love and reassurance.

Chapter Three

"I don't know why he left, honey, but I do know that people sometimes make awful mistakes, and I suspect that this is one of those times."

It is during times like these, and during conversations such as these, that trust is built and a history of intimate interaction is strengthened. Once you get beyond the chatter and get down to the heart of matters is when you begin to forge the sturdy relationships that will last a lifetime.

Breaking It Down By Age

Teens

Let's say that you are a well-respected pillar of your community, active in religious and civic groups, refined, genteel.

Let's say that your granddaughter has startling, magenta-hued hair and incredibly diverse body piercings and tattoos. You don't even want to think about the things she has pierced. Her music is loud and offensive, and she seems to spend all her time on the computer. Is there any way that you can possible connect with this foreign creature?

You can, and chances are good that the chasm you feel between you is actually no larger than the one your grandparents felt the first time you hinted that swivel-hipped Elvis was pretty cool. They were shocked, too. Remember?

We're not so naïve as to believe that there aren't very real social pressures on today's teens that can tempt them into incredibly self-destructive behavior. Casual sex and drug use are at an all-time high, and more than 70 percent of seventh graders have been drunk at least once.

Many preteens and teenagers feel adrift in our society. Parents are busy working one or two or more jobs, just to make ends meet. According to the A. C. Nielsen Co. (1998), the average American child aged two to eleven watches television 1,197 minutes per week. Meanwhile, the average number of minutes per week that parents spend in meaningful conversation with their children is 38.5.

There is a powerful void in the lives of many teens today. The time that used to be spent with parents, siblings, and extended family members is now spent at more solitary endeavors, like watching television or surfing the 'net, or maybe your teenage grandchildren join their friends at the mall, where they are surrounded by the trappings of a materialistic culture with no parental supervision or guidance whatsoever.

Off Your Rocker!
The Ultimate Guide for Grandparents

Chapter Three

So what can you, as a grandparent, do about this pathetic state of affairs?

If your grandchild comes to you with an important issue on his or her mind, then sit up straight, pay attention, and listen. Do not, under any circumstances, argue! Let your grandchild express himself fully, ask questions, share your opinion if it seems welcome, but do not allow yourself the luxury of challenging or arguing. If you do, that'll likely be the last time you're invited into such conversations.

There are more effective ways to persuade a headstrong teen. You can ask probing questions, you can ask if he considered this angle or that angle. It is generally more effective to lead someone to a conclusion than to take them there yourself. Remember the axiom: Show, don't tell.

Breaking It Down By Age

Overheard at the Mall....

On a recent shopping trip, one grandmother overheard a teenager's cell phone conversation. Having assumed that she was going to call a friend, the woman was surprised to hear this discussion:

"Hello, Mom? You won't believe what just happened! I just lost my belly ring! Can you believe it? Yes, the gold one! I know! I'm sick! Oh well, just wanted to tell you that. I love you! 'Bye!"

The grandmother was surprised by the conversation for several reasons: first, she was surprised to hear the teenager discussing so matter-of-factly something that she had assumed was a point of contention between her and her mother. Based on the conversation she just heard, apparently it was not.

Second, she was surprised to hear the teenager calling her mom just to convey information. The teenager didn't want anything. She was just telling her mom about something she felt was important.

Finally, the grandmother was surprised that, once the teenager discovered the missing belly ring, the first person she would call to tell the news would be her mother. Hmmm, she mused to herself. Must be a special relationship, indeed.

In this scenario, what appeared on the surface to be an apparent lack of parental disapproval may in fact be no such thing. The mother may abhor the belly ring, but she has done a fantastic job of keeping the lines of communication with her daughter clear and strong. And you can do the same thing with your grandchildren.

Chapter Three

Seek First to Understand

As a grandparent, it is important that you realize that your children are under tremendous pressures as parents. Being a parent today is no walk in the park. Social and financial pressures affect almost every family, and many parents today face the additional burden of single parenting. You will be a much more welcome presence in the lives of your children and grandchildren if, as Stephen Covey puts it, you "seek first to understand." This means putting your own needs, desires, and concerns aside for a while and focusing first on those of your children and grandchildren.

Carving out time to spend with a troubled teen is one of the best ways you can gain insight into his or her world. Meaningful conversations are difficult to script and plan; they tend to happen on their own, and they usually only take place in an established relationship. So, while you may not have much luck convincing your tattooed grandson that his body art looks ridiculous (at least it does to you), you might have more success in teaching him how to bait a hook. Then, while you're fiddling around by the lake, who knows what things you'll find to discuss.

Breaking It Down By Age

Give Them Space

Who knew, when the kids were small and clingy, that they would soon grow up and want nothing more than distance between them and the people who love them the most?

This is a very real, very painful phenomenon, borne out of a child's very real need to separate and form a unique identity. Thankfully, grandparents, who usually aren't as close to the grandchildren to begin with, don't experience this detachment as fully as parents do.

In many cases, the teenager finds the separation process both frightening and exhilarating, but it is during those times that the child is frightened that he often seeks out the comfort and security of someone he knows and loves and trusts, but someone who is not too close. And that would be, of course, you.

Make Yourself Available

A key to being there for your teenage grandchildren is to physically make yourself available. Have them program your phone number into their speed dialer, and make sure they know that they can call you anytime. If you live nearby, invite them over for a snack after school, or have them do their homework at your house if their parents are still at work. Invite them to join you for dinner once a week, either at your house or at a restaurant. If you live far away, make it a point to call them regularly, just to chat. Teens will drift in and out of your orbit, but when they do wander by, make sure you are there for them, sitting up straight and paying attention.

Chapter Four

So the Grandkids Are Coming for a Week... Now What?

Everybody should try to have a grandmother, especially if you don't have television, because they are the only grownups who like to spend time with us.

—from a paper written by a class of second graders

Don't let the thought of a visiting hoard of munchkins intimidate you. The key to a successful visit lies in *adequate preparation* and *realistic expectations*. Understand ahead of time that your normally pristine house will be messier than usual, and be sure to have several activities planned or ideas already worked out for things you can do together before your brood arrives.

For infants and young toddlers, you won't need anything besides a warm, soft lap and a willingness to get down on their level, both physically and mentally, to a degree. This is especially true for toddlers. If you are willing to sit on the floor or in a comfortable chair and play with small dolls or trucks for any length of time, you will be well on your way to a spectacularly successful relationship with your young grandchild.

Another key for interacting effectively with grandkids: forget the clock. Don't wear a watch. Don't be in a hurry, and don't rush from one activity to the next. You may have grand plans to take your eighteen-month-old grandson to the zoo and then out for ice cream afterwards, but if you watch him carefully you may discover that he's perfectly content to play with some new stuffed animals on your living room floor. Don't be in a rush. Go with the flow.

The Grandkids Are Coming

Making Your House a Fun Place to Visit

There's nothing tricky in making your house a place that grandchildren will enjoy visiting, but it does require a bit of advanced planning.

If you have very young grandchildren, do yourself and your kids a favor and put away any breakables or items of value. Yes, children should be taught to respect the property of others and, yes, children shouldn't touch what you tell them not to touch, but do you really want to set your house up as the measuring stick of how well behaved your grandchildren are? This is a sure-fire way to add stress to the visit.

Instead, put up the knick-knacks and let your grandchildren feel free to explore your house. Let them touch, pick up, and examine all the interesting things they'll be sure to find in an unfamiliar abode. This will serve two purposes: they will settle in and become more comfortable, and they will use this sensory exploration to learn more about you.

When Tracy A. was a child, her grandmother, who was well-traveled and liked to collect souvenirs from her journeys, would set out interesting trinkets from her travels on a small, kid-sized table. She had a carved wooden mask from the Philippines, a cast-iron replica of the Eiffel Tower, handmade beads from China, and small animals made from clay that she had collected on a trip to the Amazon. None of the items were particularly expensive, but they were kid-friendly and they gave Tracy and her grandmother a chance to discuss and "explore" together the wonderful places the trinkets represented.

In the winter months, you can take advantage of opportunities to build small, cozy traditions when your grandkids come to visit. On chilly mornings, you can lure the little ones out of bed with warm clothes fresh from the dryer, or

Chapter Four

you can similarly warm up their pajamas in the evenings before they get ready for bed. Offer them something warm to drink in the mornings when you have your coffee; herbal tea or hot chocolate will warm their bellies and their hearts at the same time.

Safety First

One grandmother, thinking she was helping, pulled her son's old walker out of the attic and plopped her twelve-month-old grandson into it while she cooked dinner. What did the kid do? He promptly rolled himself down a flight of stairs. Thankfully, the flight was a short one and the baby wasn't seriously harmed. But the incident could have been disastrous, and the end result is that none of her children feel safe using her as a babysitter.

Always make safety your primary concern when small grandchildren are coming to visit. Put away anything breakable and anything that could pose a choking hazard. Roll up cords on blinds or window treatments and fasten well above the kids' reach with twisty ties or rubber bands. Fill empty wall sockets with protective plastic plugs. And be sure to move hazardous cleaning supplies or chemicals well out of children's reach. You are probably out of the habit of constantly watching small kids, and it is all-too-easy to forget how fast and inquisitive they are. Don't tempt fate by not thinking and planning ahead for safety.

The Consistency Key

Okay then, let's look at a challenging issue: What if your grandchildren have less-than-desirable manners? What if they interrupt adults, chew with their mouths open, and tear about your lovely abode? You won't enjoy visiting with this brood much unless their behavior is brought up to a minimum acceptable standard. You can help them...really. But it does require a skillful level of tact, diplomacy, and an indefatigable sense of humor.

The Grandkids Are Coming

So, how do you teach a few manners to this unruly bunch? Start with a few ground rules. (This is where the humor comes in.) You can say with a slightly raised voice and frustration dripping in your voice, "Hey! Take off your shoes at the door, like I already told you twenty times!" Or you can say sweetly, at the beginning of the visit, "Listen, kids, I just had my carpets cleaned, so I would really appreciate it if you wouldn't wear your shoes inside the house." Then, with a sparkle in your eye, you can add: "If I catch you wearing your shoes inside, I'll confiscate your shoes and you'll have to wear my pink bunny slippers for the rest of the week!" You can even go so far as to prominently place your pink bunny slippers by the front door—a sight gag that will make the kids smile and will remind them in a nonthreatening way to take their shoes off.

If one of the kids forgets and heads for your priceless Persian rug in his mud-caked Adidas, you can stop him in his tracks with, "Oh, you must be dying to wear my bunny slippers!" At this point, he will probably smile sheepishly and take off his shoes. You will have made your point with the distinct advantage of not having been an ogre about it.

Likewise, children who interrupt can be a constant source of irritation to adults, but this maddening behavior can be thwarted with a few well-placed, kindly admonitions. And remember, urging your grandchildren to be polite will be somewhat of a lost cause if you lose your cool in the process.

If you say, "Billy, please let me finish what I am saying to my friend, then you can share your thoughts," your calm, respectful tone will reinforce the very lessons in manners that you are trying to teach.

On the other hand, you might blare, "Billy, if you interrupt me one more time I am going to…." What? Scream? Strangle him with a curtain sash? Lock him in the basement? Threats are inherently weak and ineffective. There are better ways to communicate your desires.

Chapter Four

Kids are funny. They have a way of modifying behavior based on expectations. Follow the same group of kids around at school and watch their behavior morph from class to class, teacher to teacher. The teacher who expects good behavior gets it; the teacher who has given up and thrown in the towel gets exactly what she expects: mayhem.

Set your standards high and be consistent. This is basic Parenting 101, but it has probably been many years since you've had kids in the house. The temptation is to let their behavior slide because you want to be seen as the nice grandparent—the one who bends the rules and offers bagfuls of candy and is in every other way a joy and delight to be around.

This strategy of playing to the whims of your grandkids smacks of bribery, and the truth is that children more often respect and enjoy the company of adults who bring out the best in them. So don't shy away from teaching and then reinforcing good behavior in your grandkids.

If it's been a while since you last successfully disciplined children, you may want to read up on the subject for a few reminders, tips, and pointers. (One great resource is *Positive Discipline for Preschoolers* by Jane Nelsen, Cheryl Erwin, and Roslyn Duffy.)

The Grandkids Are Coming

The Summer Vacation

While you may get to see the grandkids for a few days around the holidays, many grandparents have discovered that the real quality time is found when things are less hectic—not during the frantic winter holidays but in the slow, relaxed days of summer. Never underestimate the value of the summer vacation, even if it's only for a few days!

There are literally limitless opportunities for taking a summer vacation with grandkids. In stark contrast with the holidays, summer time spent with your grandkids can be entirely on your terms. You can invite them, you can decide where you're going, and you can decide how long the trip will last. You can have the kids stay at your house or you can go somewhere together. You can go on a modest camping trip, or you can venture to Florida or California and do the Disney thing. You can take the kids to visit great scenic travel destinations either at home or abroad. You can go on a cruise, or you can go fishing—in your backyard, in a stream down the road, or in the Great Lakes. You choose. Spending a summer vacation with the grandkids is a beautiful thing, full of potential and great experiences just waiting to be shared.

While you're planning Great Adventures to have with your grandchildren, keep in mind that what is important is the quality of the time you spend together. If you invite your grandkids to spend a week with you at your house then expect them to do nothing but watch television while you cook, clean, and work on your taxes, then your grandchildren will be (predictably) unimpressed. This is not what we mean by spending a summer vacation together.

On the other hand, a successful summer vacation with the grandkids doesn't have to cost a lot in terms of either time or money. Figure out how much time you want to spend and how much your budget will allow, then plan accordingly.

Chapter Four

A Summer Souvenir

"Why don't you take her fishing?"
I heard Grandma say, and suddenly
the world was gold and music.
I was six and grew twelve inches in an instant.
Walking riverward, Granddad hushed my chatter
with his rules for catching fish.
"One, you must be patient;
Two, you must be very quiet;
And three, you have to be a little
smarter than a fish."

Sun-spangled water purred,
rubbing its side against our sandbar.
The river smelled of wise old fish.
I weighted my feet to keep them from skipping,
tightened my lips, remembering rule two,
and wondered how one got to be
smarter than a fish.

Two fish for Grandfather later
sunshine turned from gold to heat.
Four fish for Grandfather later
I had shrunk to being six again.
Throwing caution to the ripples, I spoke,
"When are we going home, Granddad?"
He frowned and didn't answer.

The Grandkids Are Coming

Just then my line began to jerk.
I stood and pulled and tugged and strained
until I saw walking toward me from water's edge
a monstrous turtle, my hook in its mouth.
"Help, Granddad, help!" I screamed.
"Please, help me! Please!"

Trailing him home, head drooping in shame
(I'd broken them both—Rule One and Rule Two)
and knowing for certain that I'd never be
smarter than a fish.

Grandma asked how our day had gone
when Granddad handed her his catch.
"You should have been there," he said.
I turned to leave so I wouldn't hear,
but his voice grew louder as I moved away.
"She was just fine—very patient and quiet—
and while I caught only fish,
she snagged an eight-inch turtle.
And turtles, you know, are much, much
smarter than fish."

—Contributed by Phyllis Overton

Off Your Rocker!
The Ultimate Guide for Grandparents

Chapter Four

Shared Rituals

When your grandkids come to visit, look for small ways to weave meaningful moments into your interactions, even if they are seemingly insignificant. Here are a few ideas:

- Present each grandchild with his very own special drinking glass or mug to use at your house. This will not only cut down on the amount of dishwashing you have to do, but it will also give them something tangible and special to use when they come to visit. Find a mug or glass with a special design or image on it for each child: a mug with a horse on it for your granddaughter who is into horseback riding, for example, or a cup with a famous racecar driver on it for your grandson who follows racing. You can then use these special mugs for creating rituals of drinking morning beverages together, or for sharing a mug of hot cocoa in the afternoons. For older kids, you can use inexpensive wine glasses and mark each child's glass with "charms" that hang around the stem.

- If you read a newspaper, set aside interesting stories for your grandchild to read, so they can "read the paper" with you when they come to visit. Be on the lookout for uplifting stories about kids who do remarkable things, or innovations or breakthroughs in medicine or science. Then you can talk with your grandchild about these things later. "What did you think about that boy who called 9-1-1 and saved his neighbor's house from burning down?"

The Grandkids Are Coming

- Make sure to always have a couple of favorite food items or treats on hand when your grandchild comes to visit. Memories are built from repetition and consistency, so your grandchild will learn to associate these items with you. One grandmother always has chocolate chip cookies on hand; one keeps an impressive stock of Fritos in the cupboard. The particular food choice doesn't matter, though it helps if it is something that the kids enjoy!

- Develop a shared ritual of going to a certain place together. One couple loves to take their grandchildren out to a particular ice cream shop, for example; now all their grandkids think of them every time they pass a Braum's!

- Let your grandchild have "mail." Give your grandchild all your junk mail, which they can "read" as you go through your own. You may want to designate a drawer for junk mail you receive when the kids aren't there—lots of solicitations including fancy stickers, notecards, and trinkets that young children will love.

- Find small ways to build camaraderie with your grandchildren by "innocently" thwarting a few of their regular routines. Letting them have cookies for breakfast or allowing them to wear their pajamas all day or stay up past their regular bedtime won't hurt anything in the long run, but it will encourage them to love spending time with you at your house!

Chapter Four

Games to Play

"I dig being a grandmother… and of course, as a grandmother, I just run amok."

—Whoopi Goldberg

Nothing captures the attention of a young child like an adult who will play games with them. The possibilities are endless: you can rely on old favorites such as Itsy-Bitsy Spider or This Little Piggy, or you can make up your own. Tickling games are wildly popular, but keep it gentle, and remember that a little bit of gentle tickling is plenty.

For kids who are in the two to five age range, songs, singing games, and that perennial favorite Hide and Seek! should do the trick. You may want to invest in a few classic board games, too, such as Candy Land or Chutes and Ladders.

For kids ages six to nine, Checkers, Twister, and other classic board games are great to have on hand. Younger versions of classic adult games are also available, such as Monopoly Jr. and Jr. Scrabble.

For older grandchildren, consider spending an afternoon teaching a more classic game such as chess or bridge. Once your grandchildren learn classic games such as these, you will always have something challenging to do together that you both enjoy.

In the Garden

Spending time in the garden is a wonderful way to connect with your grandchildren. Have a small bucket, shovel, and kid-sized gloves waiting for them when they arrive, so they will be adequately prepared to dig and weed and putz about with you.

Designate a small area, not more than a square foot or two, as a children's garden. If you live in an apartment you can do the same thing in a large pot on the patio. If you have

The Grandkids Are Coming

several grandkids, give them each their own small plot or pot to work in.

Help the kids make a "Children's Garden" sign—a small piece of wood, a stake, and some paint is all you need. Let the kids make the sign, then teach them to till the little plot, add good soil if necessary, and take a trip to the local nursery together to select plants or seeds to put in their very own garden.

What to plant? Focus on high-yield plants that produce lots of flowers, veggies, fruit, or blooms that encourage hummingbirds or butterflies. Here are some ideas:

— Large, showy flowers such as petunias

— Watermelons

— Pumpkins

— Butterfly bushes

— Morning glories

— Sunflowers

— Vegetables

Flowers that grow quickly and yield lots of blooms are especially rewarding. Your grandkids will be amazed watching sunflowers grow, or you can help them plant vegetables and enjoy the bounty with them later on in the season. Another fun thing to do: purchase a small bag of ladybugs at your local nursery and let your grandchildren set them free in the garden.

There are many benefits to helping your grandchildren cultivate their very own "garden," even if you yourself are not a particularly avid gardener. You will have something special to do with them when they come to visit; you will teach them a skill that they will have forever (and will forever associate with you); and they will look forward to visits with you and will anticipate checking in on their plants. You can even make it a focal point in conversations you have with your grandkids on the phone: "Your tomatoes are looking lovely, Tommy!"

Chapter Four

Read, Read, Read

There's nothing like cuddling up with a loving grandparent and a good book to make children feel cherished. You're spending time with them, having physical contact, and sharing a sweet, gentle experience together. What's not to love?

With this in mind, stock up on good books before your grandchildren arrive. Take a trip to your local library, bookshop, or bargain bookstore. Good children's books are not hard to find!

If you'll be visiting your grandchildren, bring along a new book or two that you can read together and then leave with them. There are lots of great books that celebrate grandparents, and your grandchildren will think of you every time they see or read that book.

Recommended Books to Read

For a thorough list of wholesome, entertaining books for children, categorized by age, see the Appendix.

The Grandkids Are Coming

Fun in the Kitchen

The votes are in and have been tallied: No room in the house offers as much potential fun and quality bonding opportunities as the kitchen. This is the mythic room of lore, the heart of the home, the brightest and warmest room in the house, filled with comfort and good smells and delicious things to eat.

This is the room where you'll make cookies and make dinner and make memories. You'll roast turkeys and whip potatoes and hear secrets and tell stories and frost cakes and sweeten tea. The kitchen has a lot of potential for really exceptional grandparenting. Make the most of it.

If you have very young grandchildren, set aside a small drawer for kitchen items and toys that your grandkids can play with while you cook. Fill it with Tupperware containers, empty plastic food containers, wooden cooking spoons, measuring cups, and a beat-up tin pan or two. Most toy stores sell inexpensive sets of plastic "play food," so your grandkids can "cook" along with you.

Place a small stool or chair against the counter so young grandchildren can see what you're doing. Talk to them as you cook and tell them what you're doing: "Now I'll add the beaten egg whites so the cake will be nice and fluffy...."

There are some fantastic cookbooks on the market that feature simple recipes for kids. Some good ones are *The Healthy Body Cookbook: Over 50 Fun Activities and Delicious Recipes for Kids,* by Joan D'Amico and Karen Eich Drummond; and Emeril's *There's a Chef in My Soup! Recipes for the Kid in Everyone,* by Emeril Lagasse.

Chapter Four

With a little bit of advance preparation and creativity, you can use meal and snack times as great entertainment opportunities. For example, let little ones roll out canned biscuit rounds, put a spoonful of cherry pie filling in the center, fold over, and bake. After ten minutes in the oven you will have delicious "homemade" cherry pies!

Another sure-to-please recipe: **Tooty Fruity Milkshakes**. Your grandchild can help put all kinds of fruit in a blender. Bananas, blueberries, and strawberries are all great choices. Add a cup of milk, a dash of vanilla, a spoonful of sugar and some ice, and you've got a healthy snack that your grandkids will love.

For breakfast, try **Painted French Toast.** Dip slices of bread in egg, as usual, but reserve a bit of the egg mixture in small bowls and mix with food coloring. The kids can use paint brushes to add some decorative finishing touches to the toast before it is grilled or baked.

Another fun idea: **Candlestick Salad.** Set half a banana upright in a pineapple ring and "light it" with half a maraschino cherry.

The Grandkids Are Coming

You can involve grandkids in food preparation, too. Here are a few things kids can help with in the kitchen:

— Whipping potatoes
— Tearing lettuce leaves for salad
— Spreading soft cheese on crackers
— Breaking pecans
— Kneading dough
— Stirring iced tea or lemonade
   (set pitcher in the sink to prevent spills)
— Stirring batter

You can also encourage grandchildren to help prepare their own meals and snacks. Here are a few ideas:

- Set out the ingredients and let your grandkids "build" their own pizzas. You can include sliced mushrooms, bell peppers, tomatoes, pineapple, olives, pepperoni, or cooked hamburger or sausage.
- Provide bowls of fresh vegetables and let older kids put them on skewers to grill.
- Set out plates with crackers and sliced deli meats and cheese, and let kids stack and snack to their hearts' content.

Chapter Four

Kick-the-Can Ice Cream

What you'll need:
3/4 c. whole milk
1 c. cream
1/3 c. sugar
1/2 t. vanilla
2 empty, clean coffee cans (1 lb. and 3 lb.)
crushed ice
3/4 c. rock salt
masking tape
assorted flavorings of your choice (sliced strawberries, peaches or chocolate chips all work well!)

Directions:
1. In the small coffee can mix the milk, cream, sugar, vanilla and any extra items you want to add for flavor.
2. Place the lid on the can and tape it shut.
3. Put the small can inside the larger can and pack it well with crushed ice.
4. Sprinkle the salt over the ice, put the lid on the large can then tape it shut.
5. Roll (or kick!) the can back and forth for 10-15 minutes.
6. Open the cans carefully and enjoy!

The Grandkids Are Coming

Another fun, super-easy "food" project is called **Marshmallow Planet**. All you need is two bags of marshmallows—one bag of large and one bag of small, a tub of pre-made frosting, and toothpicks (can you see where we're going with this?!). Let your grandchildren build their marshmallow creations on cookie sheets, which will contain the mess. This is a good after-dinner project, when the kids will already have eaten their dinner and a few frosted marshmallows (yuck!) won't ruin their appetites. Let them build "snowmen," towers, buildings, furniture, igloos... whatever they can think of!

Chapter Four

Make Homemade Play Dough

This is the ultimate recipe for homemade play dough, and—believe me—we've tried them all. This one is quick and easy, you don't have to cook it, it doesn't stain carpets or furniture, it's non-toxic, and it doesn't smell half-bad!

What you'll need:
2 c. flour
1/3 c. salt
1 T. cream of tartar
1 T. oil
1 c. water
1 t. almond or vanilla extract

Mix together all ingredients. This dough is great for making ornaments, figurines, or just killing time on a rainy day. Younger children can manipulate the dough with spoons, forks, or straws. Kids who are a little older can use cookie cutters, dull knives, and toothpicks to embellish their works of art. If you want to harden and then paint the creations, you can bake them in a low (200 degree) oven for forty-five minutes to an hour; but be careful—they brown quickly.

For a special treat, make Peanut Butter Play Dough. Mix 1 cup peanut butter, 1/4 cup honey and enough powdered milk to make the dough smooth and kneadable. Kids can play with it like play dough and *snack* at the same time! (While the regular play dough will keep in the refrigerator for several weeks, Peanut Butter Play Dough should only be kept on hand for a few days, and always keep it refrigerated when not in use.)

The Grandkids Are Coming

While you're playing in the kitchen, stir up some imagination with this writing activity:

What you'll need: a cookbook, index cards, pencil or pen

Flip through the cookbook with your grandchild and read a few recipes together. Then have your grandchild make up a recipe for different topics, such as "Friendship," "Love," or "How to Be a Great Grandparent"!

Here's an example:

Recipe for Friendship

1 c. love

1/2 c. laughter

3 T. special secrets

1 pinch advice

Mix all ingredients; allow to marinate overnight. Eat a large helping of Friendship for lunch every day!

(Adapted from the Home & School Connection)

Chapter Four

Plan for Some Down Time

Don't feel as though you have to constantly Interact in a Meaningful Way—after all the intense fun you've been having, you both may need some down time. There are lots of high-quality children's television shows geared for young children available today. Pop in a children's video; most young children up to about age four particularly enjoy *Blue's Clues* or *Teletubbies*—then settle down with your grandchild for a little juvenile entertainment.

Your video break is a great time to offer a snack. Popcorn presents a choking hazard for small children, but you can offer goldfish crackers, dry Cheerios, Froot Loops…or make your own snacks.

There is no more sacred grandparent concept than that of baking cookies with your grandchildren. But this doesn't have to be a big deal. Young children will be thrilled with simple slice-n-bake sugar cookies: look for special themed cookies (in the refrigerated section of your grocery store) that reveal a picture when sliced. They are available year-round and are based more on seasons than holidays: in the springtime, you'll find cookies with flowers or bunnies in the center; in the summer you'll find flags. Kids love these cookies, and they are a breeze to make.

The Grandkids Are Coming

Recommended Videos to Rent or Buy

Ages Two to Five

Short videos, or those that run about twenty to forty-five minutes, are best for this age group, where attention spans can be short. Beatrix Potter has a wonderful collection of videos that feature such classic favorites as *Peter Rabbit* and *Benjamin Bunny*. The illustrations are beautiful and the messages are simple and timeless.

More current offerings include Barney (the jolly purple dinosaur), *Blue's Clues, Teletubbies, Dora the Explorer, Clifford,* and *Angelina Ballerina.* In our opinion, one of the best new lines of children's entertainment videos, books, and toys is *Veggie Tales*; the messages in *Veggie Tales* are wholesome, the characters are hilarious, and the songs are memorable.

Disney has great offerings, though they tend to have longer running times, and some may include scenes that are inappropriate for very young kids. Good ones include *The Little Mermaid, Beauty and the Beast,* and *Lady and the Tramp.* (Don't be disappointed if you can't find a particular Disney movie; certain titles are sold only at certain times, so you may want to rent the videos you want to see or look for them at your local library.)

There are plenty of kids videos to choose from; you can find them at toy stores and mass-market retailers such as Target and Wal-Mart. But buyer beware: there are plenty of videos that are marketed to young children that have no business being anywhere near children. The bottom line: if you have any reservations about what scenes or ideas or words or phrases your grandchild may digest from a particular video, it's best to watch it yourself before you plop the little ones down in front of it.

Chapter Four

Ages Six to Nine

Kids this age may enjoy watching a video as a way to work a little down time into their day. Most Disney movies are suitable, and this is the age when your grandchildren are likely to enjoy such classics as *Heidi, Mary Poppins, Charlotte's Web, The Wizard of Oz, The Sound of Music,* or *Black Beauty.* Girls will probably enjoy anything that features the Olsen twins, who are the modern equivalent of the Bobbsey Twins. Boys this age might thoroughly appreciate the antics of the Three Stooges, or even Buster Keaton or Charlie Chaplin.

Ages Ten and Up

This can be a great time to begin sharing some of your (wholesome) favorites. Kids this age may enjoy musicals or movies with deeper themes, such as *E.T. The Extra-Terrestrial, The Music Man,* or *Annie.* Other popular movies kids this age enjoy may include *Back to the Future, The Princess Bride,* and *Shrek,* which is a bit crude at times but largely a rollicking good time with a noble message.

With preteens and teenagers, you may want to consider having Movie Night, where you watch some old favorites that they may not yet have seen, such as *Casablanca* or *Gone with the Wind.*

The Grandkids Are Coming

Taming Electronic Beasts

During visits with your grandchildren, you may find your precious time with them encroached upon by a relentless, time-consuming enemy: electronics. These may take the form of e-mail or computer games; Nintendo, X-Box, or other types of video games; Game Boy or similar portable games, or even the old-fashioned television.

It is the wise grandparent indeed who figures out a proactive way to limit these electronic intrusions without seeming to be an old-fashioned meanie. Here are a few suggestions for ways you can tame the electronic beasts:

- If you only have the grandkids for a day or two, ask that they leave the electronics at home. This tactic thwarts the problem before it arises. Then, make sure you have plans for things to do with the kids that will ensure the television isn't even turned on.

- For longer visits, decide ahead of time how much time you are comfortable allowing the kids to play with or be entertained by electronics. One hour a day? Two? Next, get two clean glass jars and some buttons. Label the jars: Time Spent and Time Saved. For every half hour of time spent on the computer, watching television or playing electronic games, your grandchild moves a button from the Time Saved to the Time Spent jar. At the end of the visit, any unused buttons can be redeemed for a quarter each. (This is an especially useful tool for kids who are inclined to spend way too much time at the computer or in front of the television set. Once the buttons are gone, they're gone, and the machines are turned off.)

Off Your Rocker!
The Ultimate Guide for Grandparents

Chapter Four

- If the kids are itching for some screen action, consider getting out of the house and taking them to a movie. They get their video fix and you get to spend time doing something fun with them. Get a bucket of popcorn and settle in for some big-screen entertainment. The event becomes a shared experience, not just a time-killer.

- For younger kids, or kids ages two to five, you may want to limit time spent in front of the television to kid-friendly videos. You can rent a few so the kids will have something new to watch. As for children's television programs, beware. Just because a program is intended for young viewers doesn't mean that it will in any way correlate with values you hold dear. For younger viewers, you can safely turn on PBS, but other than that, you're on your own. There are entire networks devoted to kids that many parents won't allow their children to watch because the language is crude and the behavior displayed is inappropriate or offensive. Videos are the safer route.

The Grandkids Are Coming

Encourage Creativity

When grandchildren are headed your way, you want to make sure you have a few supplies on hand that can keep them entertained. Supplies that encourage creativity are even better! Keep a stack of clean, white drawing paper, colored craft paper, and assorted waterproof pens and markers in a drawer that your grandkids know is "theirs." Even better: put together a "Craft Box." How to assemble the perfect craft box? We'll tell you:

Assembling the Perfect Craft Box

You can pick up a plastic crate for a few dollars at stores such as K-Mart or Target. Fill the crate with craft supplies your grandkids can use when they come to visit. Toss in a few old T-shirts that they can wear to protect their clothing when they settle down for some serious creating.

After every major holiday, stock up on discounted merchandise to put in your craft box at home. Grocery stores, drug stores, and gift shops all discount holiday merchandise once the holiday has passed, so you can load up on stickers, doilies, Valentines, and whatever else that gets drastically marked down. Think of creative uses for these discounted goods.

Valentines, for example, can usually be scooped up for pennies once February 14 passes. Kids can glue them onto craft sticks to make puppets, glue them onto paper to make a collage, or use them as trading cards. You can take turns hiding them around the house, like Easter eggs. Or you can "sign" them and give them to your grandchild's stuffed animals, or put them in a paper bag (which they can then decorate) to take home to mom and dad or to give to their friends or siblings. The possibilities are endless!

Chapter Four

Shoe boxes are good; have a few set aside. Other items to put in your craft box: washable water colors, crayons, and markers; blank paper; coloring books; craft sticks; pipe cleaners; washable glue; and glitter (if you're brave). You can also stock it with items from around the house, such as old magazines, paper plates, cotton balls, pieces of string, Q-Tips, and dried beans and pasta.

What to Make

Okay, so you have all the supplies for your budding artists. What now? Here are some simple craft projects that they will love:

Collages. Kids love to make collages. These multimedia works of art can include just about anything that can be glued or taped down. You can make an "outdoor" collage that features small pebbles, leaves, flowers, or blades of grass. You can make a "face" collage out of faces that you help your grandchild cut out of an old magazine or catalogue. You could make a "food" collage out of pictures you find of food (gourmet food catalogues are great for this). Or you could make an "animal" collage or a "dog" collage or a "toy" collage. You don't even have to have a theme—you can just cut out interesting pictures and let your grandchild take his pick. (Old *Victoria* or *National Geographic* magazines are great fodder for collages, by the way; the photos are gorgeous. Watch out for old news magazines, however—the photos can be graphic.)

Puppets. Let your grandkids use old socks and pieces of felt to make puppets. The entertainment value is two-fold: they'll have fun making the puppets, then they can play with them when they're done. Use craft glue or fabric glue, and be sure to let them dry overnight before you let them play with their creations.

The Grandkids Are Coming

Shoe box scenes. Turn an old shoe box into a pretend world that you help your grandchild create! You can help them get started by spray-painting the inside and outside of a few old shoeboxes before your grandkids even arrive. Set out your craft box of supplies and let them go to town! They can create a scene out of one of their favorite books, or they can make up a scene of their own. (This can be a great place to use those old Valentines, too.)

One favorite: the Dinosaur Box. Paint the shoebox green. Use an old silk plant that has outgrown its appeal, and cut it up into small pieces of silk greenery. For the dinosaurs, use a color copier to make copies of good pictures in a book about dinosaurs from the library. Cut out the dinosaurs and glue them to pieces of shirt cardboard. Have your grandchild glue the pieces of greenery to the inside of the box. Add small stones and rocks that your grandchild finds outside. Glue the stiffened dinosaur cutouts to rocks (that are not glued down), then let the whole scene dry overnight.

For instant gratification, you can help your grandchild by using a hot glue gun; you, of course, will have to operate it, but the results are immediate. Let your grandchild decide and point to wherever they want the greenery or rocks to go, then you put them in place. Once the dinosaurs are made, they can use the scene as their very own miniature *Lost World* set. A few tips: Make sure the dinosaurs remain mobile. You want them to be able to move around the scene. And don't use dinosaurs that are too scary; you don't want this to become nightmare fodder later on in the visit!

Chapter Four

Here's a useful (and impressive) craft: custom greeting cards. You can buy blank greeting cards at craft stores and let your grandkids decorate the front, then you have customized greeting cards to use later, or they can send some to their friends.

After you have assembled the perfect craft box, turn your attention to another type of imagination-stoking device, the Dress-Up Trunk. You can buy an inexpensive plastic storage container and fill it with your old, out-of-style clothing and accessories. Shoes, scarves, shirts, vests, costume jewelry... toss it all in and watch your old castaways bring hours of entertainment to the grandkids!

You can add to the dress-up trunk periodically, and be on the lookout when you shop for fun items to add to the collection. A feather boa, veiled hat, bandanas or even a yard or two of fabric can be added now and then to keep the contents fresh and entertaining.

A word about safety: only include chains or necklaces in the dress-up box if the grandkids are over the age of five, and, if the plastic box has a lid, make sure to drill a few holes in the top, bottom, or sides of the box, just in case a little one somehow gets inside.

The Grandkids Are Coming

Get Going

If the kids get restless, here are some places you can take them for a little outing:

- A local nursery. Kids love the variety of plants, sights, and smells that are found in nurseries. Most have a gold-fish pond or garden cat hanging around, which provides even more entertainment value for your young charges.

- A library or book store. You can spend hours reading to your grandkids, looking at picture books, and browsing and looking at and feeling books of all shapes and sizes. Let them pick out a few to take home; if you are visiting the local library, they can cart home dozens of books and it won't cost a dime (as long as you return them on time).

- Go on a nature walk. See how many different varieties of bugs they can find. Take along a clean, empty jar (with a lid!) for any treasures they may find along the way, such as interesting bugs or flowers. (Many garden shops sell screened bug hotels so children can keep the insects they find in a humane, visually accessible way.)

- Visit an aquarium. This is often a better choice than the zoo—it's climate-controlled and contained in a much smaller area, which makes it easier to navigate and easier to keep track of small children.

- Are there any children's museums in your area? If so, make sure to pay them a visit. Most young kids can spend an entire day in just one section of a good children's museum.

- Have a picnic in the back yard or at a local park. Prepare finger foods, spread a blanket and enjoy the afternoon in the fresh air and sunshine. If it's particularly warm outside, let kids sit in the shelter of an umbrella (young kids love playing with umbrellas).

Chapter Four

If it's cold or raining, spread a blanket in the living room and have an indoor picnic!

- Visit a pet store. For young children, pet stores often have all the appeal of a zoo or aquarium, with the added bonus of allowing them to touch and hold some of the animals.

- Go to a craft store. For just a few dollars you can stock up on supplies that will keep your budding artists busy for hours. Be on the lookout for craft kits, which contain all the supplies you'll need (and instructions) for completing a certain craft, such as suncatchers (to hang in the window), airplanes, or beaded jewelry.

- Check out a nearby water park or amusement park. During the dog-days of summer, get out of the house and find some real excitement—amusement parks usually have rides for all ages, and water parks are great fun for older kids who can swim.

- Work on a sewing project together. If you sew, this can be a great way to spend time with your grandchildren. Take them to a fabric store and let them pick out a pattern and material, then take your treasures home and work on the project together. One great project: Halloween costumes!

Toward the end of your visit together, consider working on a small project that will document your time together. Frame a picture, make a small photo album, or write a poem that details the things you did. You want the memento to be tangible, something your grandchild can look back on that will stir his recollection of your time together.

Once the vacation is over and the kids are safely back home, you can work toward reinforcing this tremendous relationship you have started to build. Soon you can begin planning for your next visit together—after you take a good, long nap!

Chapter Five

Long-Distance Grandparenting

Absence makes the heart grow fonder.
> —Sextus Propertius (54 B.C.–A.D. 2)

When Sarah was three, her father was transferred out of state. Sarah' grandparents, Karen and Steve, had previously enjoyed a close relationship with her, but now they were terrified that, because she was so young, she would completely forget about them after the move.

They needn't have worried.

Not only had Karen and Steve—or Noni and Pops, as Sarah called them—taken the time and made the effort to connect with Sarah when she was very young, but they continued the relationship faithfully, with frequent phone calls, cards, letters, and an occasional trip.

As young Sarah grew, her relationship with her grandparents not only survived; it flourished. While they missed each other terribly, both Sarah and her grandparents continued to make the effort to stay in touch, to stay connected in spite of the miles between them. At one point Karen had an epiphany: "I realized that while I missed the day-to-day interaction, our limited time together became much more concentrated and intense. Now the highs are higher, the

Chapter Five

lows lower. We see each other infrequently, but when we do it's a smorgasbord of interaction and connection. When Sarah comes to visit me, we sleep together, eat together, play together for days. We catch up, and now our time together is so sweet and so precious that I wouldn't trade it for the world. And I now realize that we didn't have this intense time together when we lived in the same town. Then I had Sarah for much shorter periods of time. While that time was still special, our time together now has taken on a very intense, special quality."

Practical Ways to Stay in Touch

There are two variables that determine the quality of the relationship you will have with your grandchildren, and they don't change whether you live in the same house or across the country from each other. The first is the amount of time you spend with your grandchildren, and the second is the quality of time you spend with them.

Just because you live far away doesn't mean you can't spend time with your grandchildren! Frequent phone calls, letters, and e-mails can bridge the gap quite well. Even very young children can get in on the act, but you'll have to make it a conscious effort, and consistency is the key.

Long-Distance Grandparenting

Pick Up the Phone

If nothing is going well, call your grandmother or grandfather.

—Italian proverb

If you are striving for a close relationship, then phone calls should be frequent—at least once a week. Even if your grandchildren are very young, they will learn to recognize your voice. Have their parents place a photograph of you near the phone, so they can look at your picture while you talk.

When you call, remember that you are calling specifically to talk to your grandchildren. Don't make them an afterthought to a primary conversation you have with their parents. That should be a separate call. If a parent answers the phone, say, "Hello, this is Grandma calling! May I please speak to Susie?" You won't be able to see it, but on the other end of the line both the parent and the grandchild will be beaming.

Chapter Five

Talking Tips

- If your grandchildren are very young, you may find yourself unable to decipher what it is they are saying on the other end of the line. Don't worry about it. It's not so much the content of the conversation that the little ones will be jazzed about as much as the fact that they were talking on the phone! Pepper your end of the conversation with lots of comments like, "Really?" "Is that right?" and "How about that!"

- Ask lots of practical and simple questions. For very young children you can ask them things like, "What did you have for dinner tonight?" or "What is your favorite color?" Don't worry about gaps or lulls in the conversation, although if it has been several minutes since you last heard a peep from your young grandchild, you may want to consider the possibility that he put down the phone and moved on to something else entirely! Don't get your feelings hurt—this is just a function of a young, short attention span. (One grandma read a book while she waited for ten minutes for her two-year-old grandson to go to the potty and get a drink of juice, before he came back!)

- There is no rule that says you have to be serious on the phone. Sing songs, read a book together or tell your grandchild funny stories. (You may have to help a young child along with understanding what you are doing since he can't see you and use visual clues. So tell him up front, "I have a funny story for you" or "Now I'm going to sing you a silly song.")

Long-Distance Grandparenting

- For older kids you may want to consider reading the same books. Find out what your grandchild is reading, then you can read it at the same time and discuss it when you call.

- Keep the conversation centered on the child, though you may want to sprinkle in a few tidbits about yourself and your life now and then. Even young children love a conversation that includes new and interesting information. So when your grandchild tells you that he had chicken nuggets for dinner, for example, you can tell him that you had fish, then you can add that when your son—his father—was little, he hated fish! All he wanted to eat was gummy bears! You get the idea...

- Keep a calendar by the phone with lots of room to make notes, and be sure to jot down dates of upcoming events that are important to your grandchild. For example, if your granddaughter has a ballet recital coming up, then even if you are unable to attend, you can still call her on the day of the big event, or send her a small bouquet of flowers or a card to celebrate the occasion. This isn't about the gift, but it is all about being aware of and interested in the details.

Off Your Rocker!
The Ultimate Guide for Grandparents

Chapter Five

Join the Information Age

Kids today are technically savvy and often do their best communicating electronically. If you are still in the computer dark ages, sign up for a continuing education course, buy or rent a computer, and get with the program!

Many grandparents fail to understand the attraction of instant communication. Instant messaging (IM) is a mystery, while e-mail, beepers, and cell phones are just other ways that kids seem to remain distant.

This is nothing new, but the reality may surprise you: juvenile communication methods have undergone a dramatic transformation in the last few years. Just as yesterday's teens used the telephone and developed their own language adaptations ("groovy!"), today's teens IM as though their life depended on it. And here's what you need to understand: their life—their social life, at any rate—does depend on it. So don't fight this communication trend. For the most part, teens use the newest technologies to increase communication. If you can get with the program, they'll communicate with you, too.

Long-Distance Grandparenting

Here, then, are some practical ways to stay in touch with your technically savvy grandchildren:

- If you really want to keep up with your grandkids electronically and don't have a computer, you'll need to get one. Costs are coming down, and many colleges and continuing-education centers offer beginner classes.

- Get an e-mail address and use it! Keep in mind that e-mail is a much-less-formal style of communicating than traditional letter-writing. Your e-mails don't have to be long, and they don't have to be sent for any particular reason. You can easily e-mail just to say hello! (And don't forget to check your e-mail regularly for any new incoming messages.)

- Look for kid-friendly websites and send the URLs (or electronic addresses, e.g., www...) to your grandkids. A few good ones include Barbie.com, Kiddonet.com, Disney.com, and PBS.org.

- Pictures taken with a digital camera are a great way to stay in touch with your grandkids. As easy as it is to share photos over the Internet, you can share them often and for relatively insignificant reasons. You can send a photo of you making a silly face, a cake you baked, or a rainbow that you saw from your backyard. These snapshots of everyday life are a great way to stay connected, even though you may live far apart.

Chapter Five

The Value of Mail

Never underestimate the value of mail from grandma or grandpa. Children of all ages love to receive an unexpected card, letter, or silly surprise in the mailbox. Don't limit yourself to letters and postcards: use your imagination! One crafty grandma puts together a small package of craft supplies every few months and asks her grandchild to use the supplies to make her something new, then send back the finished work of art!

Another tip: For maximum impact, send packages, cards, and letters when they are least expected. For a grandchild, getting a birthday card is nice, but getting a card for no real reason at all other than to say "I love you and am thinking about you" is much more special.

While you're busy mailing, you may want to consider working on a special project with your grandchildren that you work on through the mail. For school-aged kids, you can start a silly story, for example, and take turns adding a paragraph then mailing it back and forth. Or buy a special scrapbook and take turns filling up the pages and sending it back and forth.

Make it a point to send letters frequently. They don't need to be lengthy or involved. You can draw pictures, decorate with stickers, or enclose cartoons cut from the paper. Mail from grandparents should be fun! You may want to always use the same stationery, so your letters will be instantly recognizable. In her book *How to Build the Grandma Connection*, Susan Bosak has a fantastic idea: Make photocopies of all your letters to your grandchildren and keep them in a special scrapbook. Be sure to include any letters the kids send back to you. While your grandkids probably aren't sentimental now and most of your letters to them will get thrown away, when they are older a collection of the letters you exchanged will become a priceless treasure.

Long-Distance Grandparenting

Twenty-Five Fun Things to Send in the Mail

— Silly postcards
— Stickers
— "Thinking of You" cards
— Programs or brochures from events you attend
— Small packs of gum or candy
— Baseball or other trading cards
— Articles from magazines or newspapers about things that interest your grandchild
— Seed packets
— Age-appropriate recipes
— Cassette tapes or videos on which you record songs, stories, or greetings
— An occasional dollar bill or two
— Funny pictures you find or draw yourself
— Comics clipped from the paper
— Small notepads or paperback books
— Age-appropriate magazines
— Pictures of the two of you together
— Interesting stones or feathers you find outside
— Pressed flowers or leaves
— Pictures or brochures of places you've recently visited or places you plan to visit together in the future
— Small-denomination gift certificates or gift cards to book or music stores
— Pocket-sized gift books that celebrate children
— Inexpensive faux jewelry items
— A well-wrapped batch of cookies or brownies
— Barrettes or hair clips
— Preaddressed, stamped envelopes so they can mail you letters or items in return!

Great idea: If you have school-aged grandchildren, buy a joke book and include a rib-ticker in all your cards and e-mails!

Chapter Five

Visit Often

While it's great to see the kids during the holidays, visits that occur at other times of the year are often more relaxed and less stressful. If your budget allows, visit the grandkids (and their parents!) as often as you can. Try to time your visits for highlights in your grandchildren's lives—piano recitals, championship soccer tournaments—so you will be there for their most special days.

You may be able to come only twice a year or every two months, but when you make it a point to visit frequently you accomplish several goals. You stay connected on a very real, physical level; you aren't shocked (and saddened) by dramatic changes that have taken place since you last saw them; and, most importantly, you communicate powerfully that your grandchildren are a very important part of your life. They know you love them because you make a conscious, consistent effort to see them!

When you visit often, you will soon develop patterns, visiting traditions that both you and your grandchildren love and look forward to. Maybe you'll make blueberry pancakes together the morning after your arrival, go to the zoo on sunny days to visit your favorite elephant, or go on nature walks together at a nearby park.

And here is a controversial bit of advice that we nevertheless swear by: when you visit your grandchildren, always come bearing a small gift or two! We're not talking about big or expensive gifts. Bring something small: a package of stickers, a little sack of candy, a yo-yo, a new Matchbox car, or a small freebie you got from your flight. The gift itself isn't the point; it's the fact that you thought about them in advance.

Long-Distance Grandparenting

One grandma has a small carry-on suitcase that she always takes on trips to visit her grandchildren. She uses the bag for gifts! When she arrives, the children gather around, and she makes a great show of presenting her trinkets. She brings small stuffed animals, simple blankets she made for her granddaughter's dolls, and—importantly—projects to work on together with the kids during her visit, such as craft projects or a box of cake mix.

During your visits, make sure to take lots of pictures. One grandma keeps a special scrapbook that only contains pictures and mementos from her visits with her grandchildren. She can look back through the scrapbook with them, and together they remember the special times they've shared.

The Strain of Separation

At a recent class for new mothers in a Seattle hospital, the young women were actively discussing a topic they all could relate to: grandparents. They were discussing the memories they had of their grandparents, and then they took on the topic of their own parents. What kinds of relationships did they hope to see develop between their parents and their new babies? The discussion was lively and animated.

A recurring theme soon emerged in the discussion. "I grew up in a small town where I was surrounded by my family," said one new mom. "My grandmother lived down the street, and I got to see her every day. Now my family is all spread out and we only get to see each other once or twice a year."

Chapter Five

Heads nodded in agreement throughout the room. There was a consensus. The new moms desperately missed having family nearby. They missed having their parents and siblings close by, they missed the conversation, the familiarity, and they missed the help. They wistfully discussed the relationships that they hoped they could help foster between their parents and their new babies, in spite of the physical distance between them.

The conversation continued. "What happens when grandparents live so far away?" the moderator asked.

"Well, visits become more concentrated," offered one mom. "Instead of just having dinner or babysitting for a couple of hours, when we do spend time together now it's for a whole week, which can be stressful."

More heads nodded. The fact is that when families live far apart, the visits become more intense. Stress can build. Cracks begin to show.

One Missouri grandmother, Patty, puts it this way: "When we go visit our kids and grandkids, we have to resign ourselves to countless hours of kiddie shows on television, cartons of yogurt, and deli turkey. We won't have a chance to watch the news for a week."

While there's nothing wrong with kiddie shows or yogurt, Patty has a very good point: being out of your element and suddenly living in someone else's (very different) household can be very stressful.

Long-Distance Grandparenting

Smoothing the Way

There are some basic steps you can take that will facilitate smoother visits with your brood. If there are small things that can make your visit more pleasant, then by all means mention them. For example, one grandmother mentioned to her daughter, "You know, I really love to read in bed. Do you think we could find a small lamp to put on the bedside table in the guest room?"

If you have rituals or habits that can be transported, then take them along. One grandmother loves a special flavor of coffee creamer in her morning coffee, so she buys mini packets of it before her trip and brings them along.

Another couple loves to watch a certain television show on Sunday nights. There's no harm in making such simple requests, and they can make your trip more enjoyable.

Another tip for smoother visits: keep in mind that households with young children often are not able to maintain the same standards of cleanliness to which you may have become accustomed. There may be stains on the sofa and sticky floors. The house may be crying to have its windows washed and linens changed. But here's the deal: even though you may want to help spiff things up a little, make sure your efforts won't be interpreted as a veiled criticism.

How can you make sure? Well, you could speak with your children about it. But unless they explicitly ask for your help, you run the risk of insulting them. It's better just to help clean up the daily messes that you have contributed to, such as the dirty dishes after a meal, than to roll up your sleeves and start scrubbing floors.

Chapter Five

Keep in mind that relatively small details, such as having a good reading light in the guest room or the right kind of coffee creamer, can cloud the larger, more important issues. While you may have to put up with some minor inconveniences when you visit your children and grandchildren—or when they visit you—make an effort to stay focused on the fact that the time you have with your family is limited, so you want to make it count. You want the days and hours and minutes to be filled with quality interaction and meaningful conversation, right? So who cares if the floor is sticky?

Across the Kitchen Table

My mother's mother, our Nana, lived in upstate New York while I was growing up, but she visited our family in the boot heel of Missouri each year. She arrived with stooped shoulders, black laced shoes, thick stockings, a deep voice, and a worn suitcase. She brought colorful aprons, northern cooking, and an eastern accent to deliver a story for every occasion.

Her best stories came in the morning after she drank coffee, pale and sweet with evaporated milk, as she sat at our enamel-topped kitchen table. She viewed the world in an off-center manner, and she could find redeeming value in people whose lives appeared as dull as ditch water.

Her life's work was that of a registered nurse at Pine Crest Sanatorium, a center for tuberculosis patients in New York. This specialized hospital lay tucked away from the world in a forest of pines and isolation. She worked hard and had few occasions or funds to travel to see the world. Her trips to Missouri to visit us were the extent of her travels.

Information about the world appeared to come from her intense interest in people, her observations of the details of living, and her deep love of reading and knowledge of any sort. Her storytelling was staged in our kitchen when she quieted herself to stir and sip coffee. Cup in hand, she would look across the table toward me and ask, "So, what is going on in the fourth grade?"

Long-Distance Grandparenting

The faucet dripped in the sink, but there were no other sounds in our house. It was my turn, and my grandmother listened. There was no rush. She waited for me to think and speak. She had all day, and I had this knowing that what I had to tell her was important to her. She remembered names of the kids I played with and helped me sort out daily concerns.

Nana enjoyed variety and insisted that we post a new word on the medicine cabinet mirror in the bathroom each day. And so grew my increasing love of words and their meanings. I can still see her handwriting; words she posted on scraps of notebook paper, taped to the cabinet. After a meal at our home, when my grandmother visited, I felt quite grand as I arose from the table and announced, "I am replete!" My grandmother, on hearing "today's medicine cabinet word," gave me a knowing smile. To this day, I am never full, always replete.

When I became a mother, I took my first son home for visits in my mother's home, where our Nana had moved to reside permanently. The kitchen was updated, but my grandmother stationed herself across from my three-year-old as though no seasons had changed. She was in her geography phase at this time and posted a huge map of the United States on the kitchen wall behind the table. My son sat across the table from this great-grandmother who spoke of towns and states intimately. She was heard to say, "Now here is Sikeston, Missouri. Let me tell you, that town is full of millionaires! Why, they could pave the street with cotton and dollar bills."

And when she finished yet another story and began to sip more creamy coffee, her deep musical voice continued with, "Now tell me about nursery school. Who do you play with?"

This son grew up with a great command of words and a desire to explore natural landscapes. He was also interested in inventing things that were curious and as wonderful as his great-grandmother's stories.

Today, I have a deep love and respect for language, and the stories I remember and the towns that they hold, places on the map, hold a soothing, deep voice in my head...these are the gifts from my grandmother, our beloved Nana.

—Contributed by Judith Bader Jones

Chapter Five

Go on Trips Together

When your grandchildren live far away, you can help bridge the distance gap by planning an occasional trip together—No Parents Allowed! (This is much more practical once the kids are past the toddler stage.) During the summer, you can escape with the kids for a few days or a couple of weeks, depending on the amount of time you have and your budgetary constraints.

Here are a few ideas:

Camping Adventures

If you're a camper, if you have at one time or another been camping, or if you have even a faint desire to see what all the fuss is about, then a camping vacation may be just the ticket. If you have very limited or no experience, you may want to consider a short trip; stay relatively close to home, and don't spend a lot buying expensive gear until you've gone a time or two and know that this is something you'll enjoy doing more of in the future.

Camping is one of those endeavors that can consume as much time and money as you allow. You can sleep in a tent, rent a cabin in a state park, or spend half a million dollars on a camper as big as a house.

The beauty of a camping trip is that both you and the kids get out of your element. There are no electronic distractions. You can explore your new surroundings together and figure out ways to achieve goals together ("Let's figure out the best place to build a fire," or "Let's find a good spot to go fishing!").

Long-Distance Grandparenting

The downside is that camping can be a little short on the niceties. You won't have fluffy hot towels waiting for you when you get out of the shower (if there even is one), there may be one or two bugs that share your accommodations, and you'll have trouble locating the concierge or ordering room service.

What you will find, however, is that you'll learn an awful lot about your grandkids (and probably yourself, too) in a very short period of time. You'll go exploring together, share new experiences, solve problems, enjoy nature, roast marshmallows, and tell ghost stories by the flickering glow of a campfire. You can live without pampering for a few days. You can get a good cup of coffee when you get back home.

To help you decide if a camping trip is right for you and your grandchildren, read the following statements and mark each one with which you agree:

- I love being in the great outdoors, and I'd love to share the experience with my grandchild(ren).

- It would be marvelous to have a few days in which to fully enjoy my grandkid(s) and perhaps spoil 'em a little.

- I can't imagine many more fun things to do on an outing than taking short hikes, swimming in a mountain lake, exploring an emigrant pass, taking a nap on a deck, or singing around a campfire with my grandkid(s).

- My kid(s) could sure use a break from their kid(s).

If you marked two or more of the above items, then a camping trip might be the perfect getaway for you and your grandchildren. To find out about planned outdoor camping trips for grandparents and their grandchildren, visit **www.sierraclub.com** and use the search word "grandparents."

Chapter Five

Trips Down Memory Lane

If camping isn't your thing, consider planning a trip with the grandkids to a place that is new to them but holds lots of fond memories for you. How about taking your grandson to a baseball game at the park where you saw your very first game? (This little jaunt will be even more successful if you attended your first game at Yankee Stadium!)

Find an entertaining place to visit that you remember dearly, then take your grandkids there and share the experience. What if you're an immigrant and all the action in your childhood took place halfway around the world? Be creative! If you're Italian, for example, find an authentic Italian restaurant and take your grandkids. Introduce them to new sights, sounds, and flavors. Or, if you have the time and money, take them to Italy! Which brings us to our next point:

Seeing the World

Nothing has the potential to open a child's eyes to the vast possibilities in the world around them like traveling abroad. There's just something about being in a place where the people look different, eat different food, and speak a different language, that makes the world suddenly expand. Traveling abroad for the first time is an amazing experience; it's wonderful if you can share it with your grandchild.

There are a few practical things you should consider before jetting off on an international tour. First, make sure your grandchild is old enough to actually appreciate the experience. A six-year-old probably won't be impressed by the Louvre in Paris and probably shouldn't be taken there. (However, by all means take your six-year-old to a local museum during one of your regular visits together. It's never too soon to start imparting an appreciation for the finer things in life!) It's better to wait until your grandchild is ten or so before planning an exotic trip.

Long-Distance Grandparenting

Another tip: as with all trips, make sure to consult with the parents before planning a trip abroad. In this instance, you may make an exception to the "No Parents Allowed" rule. They may be more comfortable with the idea if you go together as a family.

Honoring a grandchild's graduation, celebrating a school award, or remembering a special birthday are all terrific reasons why grandparents might suggest special trips with a grandchild. But, whether the trip is a reward, an incentive, or another expression of love, it is always and foremost precious time together.

One company that plans and coordinates both domestic and international trips for grandparents and grandchildren is called GRANDTRAVEL (www.grandtravel.com). GRAND-TRAVEL journeys provide itineraries, schedules, accommodations, and peer activities for trips that last an average of eight to fourteen days. How about a tour of the Southeast, a romp through the Pacific Northwest, or a "Castles and Kings" tour through England, Scotland, and Ireland? These trips can be expensive, but if you have a once-in-a-lifetime adventure with your grandkids in mind, this just may be the ticket. You can order a catalog of upcoming trips by calling (800) 247-7651.

Traveling with Grandchildren

There are two words you should keep in mind if you are planning to do any kind of lengthy travel with grandchildren: Be Afraid. Actually, we're just kidding—well, sort of. Here are the two words you really need to keep in mind: Be Prepared. If you're not prepared, then you can go ahead and be afraid, because there is not much worse in the world than being contained in a small space with bored, cranky kids. It's kind of like torture.

Chapter Five

So, the key to traveling with your grandchildren is being prepared. What does this mean? We'll tell you.

You will need to prepare differently for kids of different ages, but first we'll run down the basics. In a nutshell, no matter what the age, you want to do everything in your power to keep the little darlings comfortable, fed, and entertained.

This is not as easy as it sounds.

In general, an inverse relationship exists as to the size of the child and the amount of stuff they'll need to bring along. For babies, you'll need bottles, diapers, wipes, extra clothes, a car seat and infant carrier, toys, books, and teethers. A teenager, on the other hand, may just need frequent stops for fast food and a new CD or two to pop into his Walkman.

If you are planning on traveling with small children, then plan travel time to coincide, as much as possible, with their regular nap schedule. If they can sleep in the car, on the train or on the plane, the trip will go by much faster (for them and for you).

Something else to keep in mind: whether or not your grandchildren travel well depends to a large degree upon their temperaments. Some kids travel well; others do not. Some can sit, perfectly content, in a car seat for hour after hour, while others will be squirming and whining after ten minutes of such confinement.

If your grandkids do travel well, by all means, take them along wherever you want to go. If they don't, that's okay, too; but you may not be so quick to volunteer to take them on a car trip to Disney (when you live in Dallas), if that is the case.

Chapter Six

Happy Holidays

Grandmothers preside over the great family festivals and celebrations—Christmas, Easter, Yom Kippur, Hanukkah. They bind us to the great occasions of life....

—Page Smith,
from *Old Age Is Another Country*

The holidays have arrived, the tree is up, the lists are made, and the baking has begun. This is not the time to forge strong emotional ties with your offspring, to have deep meaningful conversations that tap into your souls and bind you together forever. Instead, this is the time to make happy memories, to get lost in a brightly hued world of tinsel and merriment, to teach your grandkids to make cutout cookies and perfect gravy, and to watch the sky for signs of a jolly little man dressed in red.

Chapter Six

Building Traditions

When Rachel, who is seven, goes to visit her father's parents during the holidays, she looks forward to going to Midnight Mass. Rachel's parents don't attend church regularly, and Rachel has no particular desire to go to church at other times during the year, but when her extended family bundles up to head for the yearly late-night Christmas Eve service, Rachel's heart does a little leap. It's one of her favorite things about the holidays.

Predictability and repetition are the keys to building long-term family traditions. In many cases the family is not even consciously going about developing a "tradition"; it just happens.

One family grew accustomed to having sour cream dip and chips served in a garish orange serving bowl at family get-togethers. The bowl and dip and chips were there at every family gathering, and it soon became a fixture, a beloved, tacky tradition. Now the bowl is there for every occasion, set with pride and a sense of humor among the china and crystal for holiday feasts.

Traditions can be small and simple or grand and elaborate. What you eat, where you go, what you wear, where you sit, and even what you say can all gel and form an environment that is filled with familiarity and meaning.

One grandpa regularly squeezes his grandchildren's pinkies when he sees them. He does it all the time, every time, and the kids have grown to expect and love his little tweaks.

One grandma always bakes fresh banana bread on the day after Christmas.

Happy Holidays

One couple invites the entire family over for turkey pot pie a few days after Christmas. The kids bring their new toys, and the parents have a chance to relax and catch up with the rest of the family without having a huge, elaborate meal to prepare or a bazillion gifts to unwrap.

Take some time to think through traditions you would like to help develop for your family and for your grandchildren. Try to keep them simple and easy to duplicate, something your grandkids can remember and repeat when they are older and have families of their own. A favorite recipe, a special song, or an event that is revered (such as Midnight Mass) all have the potential to become cherished holiday traditions for you and your family.

Grand Holiday Traditions to Develop with Your Grandchildren

- Dressing up and going to see *The Nutcracker*
- Visiting the zoo together on the day after Christmas
- Taking homemade holiday cookies to a local hospital or retirement center
- Buying (or making) presents, then wrapping them together to give to your grandchild's parents—your child(ren)!
- Singing Christmas carols or holiday songs together
- Watching a classic holiday film together every year, such as *It's a Wonderful Life* or *Charlie Brown's Christmas*
- Participating together in a giving program where you select a toy for a less fortunate child and donate it (many churches, synagogues, and even shopping malls sponsor these programs)
- Building a gingerbread house together

Off Your Rocker!
The Ultimate Guide for Grandparents

Chapter Six

Easy Holiday Recipes and Crafts

While we want to make every effort to keep this from becoming another recipe-and-craft book, we have found a few tried-and-true recipes and crafts that are simple, require few ingredients, and provide lots of fun, quality time with the grandkids. You don't need a whole book full of ideas—just a few good ones! Here are some of our favorites:

Recipes

Citrus-Coconut Balls

These delicious holiday treats are fun to make and even more fun to eat. Help your grandchildren assemble the ingredients, then let them make the balls and roll them in coconut.

You'll need:

1 box vanilla wafer cookies, crushed

1 stick butter, melted

2 c. powdered sugar

1 small container frozen orange juice concentrate (or limeade or other citrus beverage), thawed

1 c. finely chopped pecans, toasted

1 t. vanilla

2 c. shredded coconut

Crushing the vanilla wafer cookies and/or pecans is a great job for small hands. Put the cookies and toasted pecans in a large zip-lock bag and have your grandchild crush them with the back of an ice cream scoop. You can also use a food processor, but the sanctioned banging and whacking and crushing to small bits is great fun for the little ones. In a large mixing bowl, mix all ingredients except the coconut. Roll mixture into small balls then roll in coconut. These cookies are much better after a day or two—they are perfect for boxing up in cookie tins to give to the neighbors or your grandchild's teacher.

Happy Holidays

Hello, Dollies!

These classic layer cookies are good for even small children to help make.

What you'll need:

2 c. crushed graham cracker crumbs

1/2 c. butter, melted

1 bag chocolate chips, 12 oz.

1 c. shredded coconut

1 c. chopped pecans

1 can sweetened condensed milk

Mix the graham cracker crumbs with the butter then press into 8 x 8 baking pan. Bake at 350 for 10 minutes, or until set. Let cool until warm—not hot enough to burn a small helper! Layer chocolate chips, coconut, and pecans over crust. Pat down lightly, then pour can of sweetened condensed milk over all. Bake at 350 for 30 minutes. Let cool, then slice into squares. These are rich cookies—we suggest slicing them into small squares then serving with tall glasses of cold milk!

Crazy Chex

Another classic holiday recipe that kids love to bake (and eat!). Follow the recipe on the back of any box of Chex breakfast cereal, but you can be creative with what you choose to add. For example, instead of regular pretzel straws, look for pretzels in fun, kid-friendly shapes. You can toss in a few "baby goldfish" crackers, too!

Chapter Six

Macadamia French Toast Casserole

This simple, delicious recipe is easy to make—even small children can help. Assemble it the night before, refrigerate the casserole overnight, then pop it the oven first thing in the morning. The whole house will smell wonderful as it bakes, and you won't have to lift a finger. (This is also a great recipe for brunch.)

> 1 loaf fresh French bread, sliced into 1-inch slices (ends removed)
> 5 eggs, lightly beaten
> 4 T. butter, melted
> 1/2 cup whole milk
> 1/2 cup orange juice
> 1 t. vanilla
> 1/2 c. sugar

Lay slices of French bread flat in a greased casserole dish. Whisk other ingredients then pour over slices of bread. Cover with foil and refrigerate overnight.

When you're ready to bake the casserole, remove the foil, put the casserole in a cold oven, then heat to 350. Bake 40-45 minutes, or until French toast is golden brown.

For topping: Lightly toast 1 cup crushed macadamia nuts and 1/2 cup coconut. Sprinkle over baked French toast, then serve with warmed syrup and fresh orange slices.

Happy Holidays

Crafts

The holidays provide an ideal time and occasion for whole-hearted creativity. It's cold outside, so indoor activities beckon. Light a fire, make some hot cocoa, and let the creative spirit loose!

Crafts need not be tied to a specific holiday theme. Plain white printer paper can be put to good use as "snowflake" material. Fold the paper into quarters and let the cutting begin!

Check to see if there is a pottery store in your town. If you have the kids a few weeks (or months) before the official holidays begin, take them to the store and let them paint their own ornaments, or decorate plates or mugs with their handprints. These make great presents for their parents, who will be both thrilled and surprised at the quality and innovation of the gifts "from the kids"!

You'll be way ahead of the game if you can figure out a way to have your grandchildren make crafts that you can use later for another purpose. Two classic examples include holiday greeting cards and salt dough ornaments.

Greeting Cards

For the ultimate holiday greeting card, have someone take pictures of you with all your grandchildren, if possible, when you all get together to celebrate Thanksgiving. You're all dressed up, everyone is there, and the photo will be recent. You can glue the photo on the outside of a card, or put it inside the card, or buy cards that have a special place to insert the photo. The possibilities are endless!

You can buy blank cards at craft shops, office supply stores, and some specialty card stores. Set out some newspaper, washable tempera paints, rolls of paper towels, and paintbrushes, and then stand back and let your grandchildren use their holiday-inspired imaginations!

Chapter Six

For very young children, you can trace the circle of a drinking glass on the card, then let your grandchild dip his finger in paint and then follow the circle, making a "fingerprint wreath." Once the paint is dry, you can glue a small bow on the top of the wreath and voila! You have gorgeous, handmade cards to send to friends or family.

Classic Salt Dough Ornaments

This smooth, impossibly easy dough will yield perfect, paintable ornaments every time. Just don't eat the dough!

2 cups flour

1 cup salt

1 cup warm water

Preheat oven to 325. Mix ingredients together until dough forms a loose ball; turn out and knead 8-10 minutes or until smooth. (Kids over the age of about four can be great at kneading.) Shape dough into any shape you desire: you can use cookie cutters, dull knives, toothpicks, fork tines, anything you can think of to make anything you want!

Happy Holidays

Here are a few ideas for things you can make with salt dough:

— Snowmen

— Angels

— Wreaths (braided wreaths are especially nice)

— Miniature nativity figurines

— "Fruits" and "vegetables"

— Letters, numbers, and shapes

— Hollow circles or squares you can later make into picture frames

Use the end of a straw to punch holes in the tops of the ornaments you will want to hang later. (Once they're baked it's too late to make holes.) Bake your creations at 325 for 45 minutes to an hour. Watch the ornaments carefully; if the oven is too hot they will brown too quickly. (If the ornaments do get overly brown, all is not lost—these just become "gingerbread" ornaments!)

Once the ornaments are done, let them cool, then decorate. You can use regular water-based tempera paints, glue, and edible cookie decorations, glitter or glitter paint… once again, you are only limited by your imagination. After the décor is dry, you may want to varnish your finished creations so they will be shiny and last a long, long time.

Once the varnish is dry, tie on cheerful ribbons for hanging. You'll be amazed at how easy these are to make, and how beautiful and nostalgic-looking they are once they're done.

Chapter Six

Decorating with the Grandkids

If you have a Christmas village, nativity scene, menorah, or other holiday symbol, let your grandchildren help set it up. Even small kids can help add "snow" to scenes or set up unbreakables.

If your decorative scenes are expensive or breakable, many craft stores sell inexpensive versions of the classic holiday decorations; consider buying a spare so the kids can set up their own. This activity also provides a great way to teach the children about their heritage, to tell them stories about your childhood, and share stories about your faith or your beliefs.

If you have the space, a small Christmas tree can be set up in a corner. This "Children's Tree" can be just for the kids, and they can make decorations to put on "their tree."

You can set aside unbreakable décor items just for the kids to put up when they come to visit. Older kids can be tapped for creating a dining room table centerpiece with materials you provide. Younger kids can string popcorn or dried cranberries.

(One of the benefits of having your grandchildren help you decorate for the holidays is the unexpected moments of pleasure and surprise you'll have once the kids have gone home and you have a chance to take a better look around. One grandmother discovered that her grandchild had wrapped the baby Jesus in a fabric scrap when she set up the manger scene; another grandma found that her grandchild had put a candy cane in the cup where she kept her toothbrush!)

Happy Holidays

As much as possible, include your grandchildren in other types of holiday preparations, too. Plan ahead of time to have suitable chores for each of the kids. A six-year-old, for example, will set the table beautifully (do bite your tongue if the forks appear out of order or an occasional knife is upside down!). Grandkids can help shell peas, crack and hull pecans, knead bread dough, or arrange fruit and vegetables on a tray.

Older grandchildren can be enlisted to help prepare pies, chop vegetables, whip potatoes, or add sugar to tea. Use this opportunity to encourage your grandkids to become comfortable around the kitchen. (One thinking grandma had her teenage granddaughter come for a sleepover a few weeks before the holidays. She taught her granddaughter how to make a pumpkin pie that night, then put her in charge of the pie a few weeks later.)

To help keep the kids entertained, set up a small card table in an out-of-the-way corner and have it supplied with prebaked cutout sugar cookies, frosting, and decorations, then have the kids make their own "dessert." One creative grandmother baked and assembled a gingerbread house (you can even use a hot glue gun), then let her grandchildren decorate it with frosting and hard candies while she worked on preparing the holiday meal. (You can modify this idea and use a ready-made gingerbread house kit, which is seasonally available in many grocery stores.)

Another inventive grandmother hides pennies throughout the house (but not in the kitchen!) before her grandchildren arrive. Later, the child who finds the most pennies wins a small prize.

Chapter Six

Along those same lines, if the weather cooperates, consider hiding small trinkets outside in the yard (but only if the yard is enclosed and there is no swimming pool or other obvious hazard).

If you have several grandchildren, put them in charge of the evening's entertainment. This instruction usually sends the brood scurrying off to a spare bedroom to plan and practice a "skit" or "variety show." This is a great idea for two reasons: it gets the kids out from under your feet while you are trying to put a big meal together, and then, once the meal is finished, you can all sit back and be entertained by your performing darlings. And don't forget the video camera! (Once this tradition takes on a life of its own and the kids really get into it, consider giving them an "early" gift of a karaoke machine, to enhance their performances!)

Happy Holidays

Gift Giving Gone Awry

In many cases, along with the frenzied merriment of the season comes a pressure to buy gifts. Lots and lots of gifts for lots and lots of people. It can seem overwhelming. Deciding what to buy for whom can soon begin to feel like a chore, one more thing to have to do, an item to get crossed off your too-long list.

Many grandparents have succumbed to the temptation of finding a suitable, generic gift and buying it in bulk for their grandchildren, cloaking it with the virtuous-sounding disclaimer that "we want to treat all the kids the same."

It is true that this form of gift-buying makes all the kids feel the same. But is this really the way you want them to feel...as if you *had* to buy their gifts and were so inconvenienced by the task that you took the easy way, the path of least resistance? Yes, all the grandchildren will feel the same, all right.

Sara was nineteen when her grandmother became sick. Diagnosed with cancer, she fought it bravely for well over a year. Sara had enjoyed a close relationship with her grandmother. The holidays were always a special time, and her grandmother enjoyed giving small, meaningful gifts to each of her four grandkids. "I knew my grandmother was really sick the year she gave us all the same Christmas gifts," says Sara. "She told us all to wait, to open our gifts at the same time, and we looked at each other and suddenly realized that if she gave us all the same gift, she was really not feeling well."

Off Your Rocker!
The Ultimate Guide for Grandparents

Chapter Six

There is an exception to the idea of mass, generic gift-buying for the grandkids, however. Kudos to you if you are buying the same gift for all the grandkids that serves to bind them closer to you, or to share a part of yourself with them. If you are an avid fisherman, for example, then buying fishing rods for each of the grandkids is a thoughtful, meaningful gift. Or if you love to garden, then giving each grandchild their own set of gardening tools to use at your house is a great way to make them feel special and share your passion.

So, when it comes to buying gifts for the holidays, here is an opportunity, a chance to flex your well-toned grandparenting muscles.

Remember the Grandparent's Notebook, the loose-leaf binder we talked about in Chapter 1? This is the book where you keep a section on each child, where you record the names of their friends and teachers, their likes and dislikes, the foods they especially enjoy, the music they listen to, and the books they like to read. This is your cheat-sheet, a way to keep track of the myriad details, a way to chronicle and record the details about your grandchildren that you otherwise might forget.

If you have maintained your Grandparent's Notebook, you'll be well on your way to making holiday gift buying a breeze. You can flip through the book, taking note of special interests, hobbies, or collections; then make a list, and rest assured that the gifts you buy for your grandchildren will be thoughtful and appropriate.

Happy Holidays

Even if you have a large brood, you can still give personal gifts, though it might simplify matters to give gifts according to a general theme. For example, if you have ten grandchildren and want to spend twenty dollars or less on each grandchild, you might want to choose an outdoor theme and give toys that can be played with outdoors. Make a list of the kids and their ages and head to Target or Wal-Mart, where you'll find something for everyone.

Your list might look something like this:

John (2) — rubber ball

Susan (3) — plastic bucket and pail

Robert (4) — dump truck

A.J. (5) — Matchbox cars and ramp

Marshall and Jenny (6) — bug catchers or ant farms

Mitchell (9) — a kite

Lauren (10) — garden tools with seeds and a pot

Alexa (12) — sunglasses

Liam (14) — a baseball cap with the logo of his favorite team

It is much more meaningful to give individual gifts; don't worry if the gifts don't cost exactly the same. Some years what you give the kids will be more of a hit than others. Robert may love his dump truck one year but not be so jazzed about the baseball you give him the next. You can't win 'em all!

Chapter Six

While you're buying gifts for the grandkids, consider giving a gift to your child and his or her spouse that will let them have a bit of a break from the constant requirements of caring for children. If you can afford it, give them a gift certificate to a nearby hotel and a coupon for babysitting; they get away for a night or two and you get to spend some quality time with your grandkids.

If the parents seem particularly worn down, consider giving them a coupon book with lots of guaranteed babysitting offers. "This coupon good for two hours of free babysitting," "This coupon good for one night's stay at grandma's," "This coupon good for movie tickets, popcorn, and free babysitting"… you get the picture.

Jingle-Jangled Nerves?

There is a tendency in all of us (or many of us, anyway) to become overwhelmed by the demands of the holidays. What starts out as lighthearted fun can soon snowball into a required whirlwind of shopping, cooking, and entertaining, to the point of exhaustion. At times such as these, the presence of young grandchildren underfoot can be—how to put this delicately—*stressful*.

These are the times when it is important to take a long-term view of the situation. It's easy to be a calm, loving grandparent when a baby sleeps peacefully in your arms on a quiet weekday morning. Being such a paragon of virtue is another matter entirely when the turkey is burning, the gravy is scalding, the mashed potatoes have lumps, older grandkids are whining to open their gifts, and the baby won't stop squalling.

Ah, yes, the long-term view.

Happy Holidays

When you feel the stress starting to mount and your blood pressure beginning to rise, take stock of the situation and remember what is truly important about the holidays. Does anybody really care about whether the turkey is a wee bit dry? If the baby is crying, the baby's mother is probably stressed, too. What to do, what to do?

Take a deep breath. Have a glass of wine or a cup of tea, if that soothes you. Put on some low, soothing music. Designate chores in the kitchen. Have an older grandchild whip the lumps out of the potatoes. Use a jar of gravy if you must. Take the bird out of the oven and relax. The rest of the family will follow your lead.

If the meal is an unmitigated disaster, go out for Chinese. Or eat the burned bird anyway and chalk it up to a celebration of wonderful company and not-so-wonderful food. Help the parents calm the screeching infant; let the children open and play with their toys.

When all else fails, remember that the holidays are meant for spending time with our loved ones and reconnecting after weeks and maybe even months apart. The ultimate goal here, the golden ring, is to find the humor in the situation and remember to laugh. When the day is over and everyone goes home, what they will remember isn't the perfect potatoes, but whether or not they enjoyed the visit and had fun seeing the rest of the family. The food is not the point. The family is.

Off Your Rocker!
The Ultimate Guide for Grandparents

Chapter Six

A Christmas to Remember

I remember my first Christmas adventure with Grandma. I was just a kid. I remember tearing across town on my bike to visit her after my big sister dropped the bomb: "There is no Santa Claus," she jeered. "Even dummies know that!"

My Grandma was not gushy, never had been. I fled to her and knew she would be straight with me. Grandma always told the truth, and I knew that the truth went down a lot easier with one of her world-famous cinnamon buns. (I knew they were world-famous, because she said so.)

Grandma was home, and the buns were still warm. Between bites, I told her everything. She was ready for me. "No Santa Claus!" she snorted. "Ridiculous! Don't believe it. That rumor has been going around for years, and it makes me mad, plain mad. Now, put on your coat, and let's go."

"Go? Go where, Grandma?" I hadn't even finished my second bun.

"Where" turned out to be Kerby's General Store, the store that had a little bit of everything. As we walked through its doors, Grandma handed me $10. That was a bundle in those days. "Take this money," she said, "and buy something for some-one who needs it. I'll wait for you in the car." Then she turned and walked out of Kerby's.

I was only eight years old. I'd often gone shopping with my mother, but never had I shopped for anything all by myself. The store seemed big and crowded, full of people scrambling to fin-ish their Christmas shopping. For a few moments I just stood there, confused, clutching that $10 bill, wondering what to buy, and who on earth to buy it for. I thought of everybody I knew:

Happy Holidays

my family, my friends, my neighbors, the kids at school, the people who went to my church. I was just about thought out, when suddenly I thought of Bobby Decker. He was a kid with bad breath and messy hair, and he sat right behind me in Mrs. Pollock's second grade class. Bobby Decker didn't have a coat. I knew that because he never went out for recess during the winter. His mother always wrote a note, telling the teacher that he had a cough, but we all knew that he didn't have a cough; he didn't have a coat. I fingered the ten dollar bill with growing excitement. I would buy Bobby Decker a coat!

I settled on a red corduroy one with a hood on it. It looked warm, and I thought he would like it. "Is this a Christmas present for someone?" the lady behind the counter asked kindly, as I laid my money on the counter. "Yes," I replied shyly. "It's for Bobby." The nice lady smiled at me. I didn't get any change, but she put the coat in a bag and wished me a Merry Christmas.

That evening, Grandma helped me wrap the coat in Christmas paper and ribbons. (A little tag fell out of the coat, and Grandma tucked it in her Bible.) "Now write 'To Bobby, From Santa Claus' on it," Grandma said, "Santa always insists on secrecy." Then she drove me to Bobby Decker's house, explaining as we went that I was now and forever officially one of Santa's helpers. Grandma parked down the street from Bobby's house, and she and I crept noiselessly and hid in the bushes by his front walk. Then Grandma gave me a nudge. "All right, Santa Claus," she whispered, "get going."

I took a deep breath, dashed for his front door, set the present down on his step, rang the doorbell and flew back to the bushes with Grandma. Together we waited breathlessly in the darkness for the front door to open. Finally it did, and there stood Bobby.

Chapter Six

Fifty years haven't dimmed the thrill of those moments spent shivering, beside my Grandma, in Bobby Decker's bushes. That night, I realized those awful rumors about Santa Claus were just what Grandma said they were: ridiculous! Santa was alive and well, and we were on his team. I still have the Bible, with the tag tucked inside: $19.95.

—Author unknown

Chapter Seven

Grandparenting 9-1-1

Grandmothers are very good at picking up the pieces of something shattered beyond all mending—and mending it.

—Clara Ortega

Studies in recent years have shown that grandparents—maternal grandmothers, in particular—have a powerful role in the lives of their grandchildren. In impoverished regions of the world, in fact, the presence of the maternal grandmother often means the difference between whether or not the grandchildren survive—literally. When times are hard, grandparents can step in and help. It is this realization that can enable grandparents to rise above difficulties and reach out to help despite circumstances.

In this chapter, we will examine some of the larger issues that may loom in your relationship with your grandchild. Maybe you are sick, maybe your grandchild's parents are divorced, maybe your grandchild is having difficulty in school or a hard time making friends. None of these difficulties are uncommon, and there are lots of ways to effectively work around the problems you may face.

Chapter Seven

When trouble looms, the primary messages you want to convey to your grandchild are that you love them unconditionally and that you are there for them. Tape these words to your bathroom mirror if you must, but keep them in mind. Sure, when times are great, grandparents can be a lot of fun, but it is when times are tough that many grandparents step into a fuller role and really begin to shine.

Pitfalls, Traps, and Larger Issues

"I can't be an effective grandparent because...." Ever found yourself thinking that the tasks involved in quality grandparenting are just too difficult? Well, join the crowd. Just like any other significant endeavor, there are times when being an effective grandparent will be tough.

What, you'd rather go shopping or have lunch with friends than stay home babysitting a colicky infant so your daughter can finally get some sleep?

You'd rather go fishing alone than take along a rambunctious five-year-old who is guaranteed to do nothing but frighten away every fish within a two-mile radius of your boat?

It is a little-acknowledged fact that grandparenting—like parenting—can be tough. The demands that a child makes can be relentless. As one grandfather says, "It wasn't until I became a grandfather that I fully realized that it takes two generations to raise one." This grandfather realized how much his kids needed help once he saw from a somewhat objective point of view how difficult it can be to raise infants, toddlers, and eventually teens.

Grandparenting 9-1-1

Coming to terms with the fact that helping your kids raise theirs isn't guaranteed to be all sweetness and light is likely to seriously alter any unrealistic grandparenting expectations you may have, but don't despair—this is a good thing. Just like any other relationship, your relationship with your grandchild is only improved by having realistic expectations.

Remember to Laugh

This probably will come as no surprise, but the key to smoothing out the rough spots with your grandchildren, your children, and any difficulties that occur within these relationships lies in keeping your sense of humor.

One grandma was thrilled at the prospect of helping to bathe her year-old granddaughter. Washing that little fuzzy head with warm soapy bubbles and playing with rubber duckies had enormous appeal... until the baby pooped in the tub. "I had forgotten that babies sometimes do that!" she said later with a somewhat sheepish smile. At that point, grandma had two options—she could be visibly disgusted, or she could laugh at the situation and help her flustered daughter clean things up.

Perhaps your teenage grandchildren are going through "an experimental" stage. You may not prefer multiple piercings or nontraditionally hued hair color, but try to keep these things in perspective. Most teens outgrow the need to demonstrate outward signs of rebellion or nonconformity, and if you are able to love them unconditionally through these stages, you may very well find yourself rewarded in the end. (In many cases, children who go through difficult teenage years find that they are able to trust and talk to their grandparents when discussions are too volatile with their parents.)

Chapter Seven

Developing realistic expectations carries over into what you expect from your kids and their spouses, too. Keeping your mouth shut, for example, can be enormously challenging when you see your son or your daughter or either of their spouses making what in your opinion is a mistake—especially if you made that same mistake in your own life.

"It was enormously liberating for me to realize that people learn best from their own mistakes," says one grandfather of five. "Once I realized that it really is not my position to point out mistakes, I could relax. I learned from my mistakes, and I'm reasonably certain that my kids and my grandchildren will learn from their mistakes. My kids used to call me the 'Policeman of the Universe.' Once I gave up that role, our relations became much smoother."

Grandparenting 9-1-1

How to Help a Struggling Grandchild

Witnessing the struggles of your grandchildren can be painful. What if they have very few friends, or worse, what if the friends they do have look like real trouble?

While there are no easy answers to these questions, what remains fundamentally important is that your grandchildren see you as a source of unconditional love and support. While you may not agree with the decisions your grandchildren make, you can still show that you care about them and want to be a part of their lives.

This is especially true for grandchildren in their teenage years. While teens may appear to be aloof and disaffected, at our core all of us want to be loved, appreciated, and listened to—teenagers included.

Maintaining a relationship with a struggling teen will take effort. And time. You will not have a strong, special bond with a disaffected teenage grandchild that you see only at Thanksgiving and Christmas. But take this same struggling child out for coffee once a week and the situation—and the bond between you—will be entirely different.

"Amount of contact and frequency of contact between grandparents and grandchildren are pretty critical variables to consider," says Professor Patricia Jarvis, a professor of psychology at Illinois State University, who has studied the relationships between grandparents and grandchildren extensively.

The short answer, then, to helping a struggling grandchild? Be there. Talk to him, and listen to him. Be a friend.

Chapter Seven

Traps to Avoid

There are a few predictable areas where some grandparents run into trouble. While this list of inaccurate or destructive thoughts, feelings, beliefs, and gestures is by no means exhaustive, it may help shed some light on some of your own areas of difficulty in your relationships with your grandchildren:

- Assuming that your grandchildren don't want to spend time with you. The fact is that most grandchildren crave time with the adults in their lives that they know and trust. Your presence can reassure your grandchildren, from infants to teens. In addition, studies show that the more time children spend with their grandparents, the more they respect older people, and the less fear they have of growing older.

- Not recognizing the important role you can play in the lives of your grandchildren. Children look to adults for guidance not only in important matters of identity and morality but also in more mundane ways. Your interests can guide and shape your grandchildren in ways you probably will never know. For example, Gina's grandmother was an avid gardener. As a child, Gina spent hours with her grandmother in the garden— weeding, pruning, and learning about how and why things grow the way they do. As a teen and young adult, the garden held little appeal for Gina, but as an adult, once she owned a house and a little plot of land all her own, the things she learned from her grandmother in the garden so many years earlier came rushing back. Today Gina spends many fulfilling hours in her beautiful backyard sanctuary, and she gives her grandmother all the credit.

Grandparenting 9-1-1

- Thinking that you have to have a lot of money or material possessions in order to be appealing to your grandchildren. What is important to children is the fact that you spend time with them when you are able, and the knowledge that you care about them and think about them on a regular basis.

- Talking down to or underestimating your grandkids. Children in our society tend to grow up faster than children in previous generations; their emotional levels of maturity and awareness are often more sophisticated than you would expect. Try to incorporate this knowledge into your interactions with your grandkids. Ask questions, and keep an open mind.

- Not sharing the details of your life with your grandkids. Teaching your grandchildren how to cook or fish or sew is great; these are skills they will use and appreciate. However, with older and more mature grandchildren, the day that you let down your guard and share with them a personal problem or issue that is affecting you is the day that your relationship gets taken to a deeper, more emotionally satisfying level. For example, Janet began to see her grandmother through new, more appreciative eyes when her grandmother admitted to her that her relationship with her grandfather had not always been as easy at it appears. Janet's parents were smack in the middle of some pretty hair-raising marital turmoil, and Janet was scared and worried. Her grandmother's stories of how she and Janet's grandfather had eventually resolved their conflicts soothed Janet and calmed her fears.

Chapter Seven

- Feeling like you have to compete with the other set(s) of grandparents. Many grandparents feel a sense of competition with the other grandparents, though the truth is that children accept the individual family members as just that: individuals. Grandparents are what they are, and most children find a way to mentally identify each grandparent based upon what they have experienced with that grandparent, as opposed to identifying them in relation to other grandparents. For example, seven-year-old Susan has a grandmother who loves cats and a grandmother who loves to go to church and a grandmother who loves the outdoors. There is no value judgement in any of those "labels." There are no favorites, just differences.

- Being ashamed of past failures in your life around your grandkids. There is a tendency to believe that our children and grandchildren will evaluate us based on our past mistakes, so mistakes should be minimized. While you may not want to aggrandize the scope of your past failures, sharing them with your grandchildren will demonstrate to them that you are humble and willing to confront your past honestly. Allow your grandchildren to learn from your past mistakes and learn that wisdom often comes as the result of having made mistakes.

Grandparenting 9-1-1

- Not "picking your spots" carefully. One well-meaning grandmother, who had lived through the Depression and was relentlessly frugal as a result, used to constantly admonish her granddaughters to use only four sheets of tissue paper when they used the bathroom. "I hear her in my head every time I go to the bathroom," her now-grown granddaughter says. "'No one needs more than four squares'!" Is this really how you want to be remembered?

- Assuming the role of Family Protector. Many well-meaning grandparents assume that the family will fall apart if they fail to intervene. As a result, they become busybodies, probing and asking nosy questions, then passing along the information to other family members in an effort to keep the rest of the family "informed" or "up to date." This is a dangerous role to play: if you are always talking about other family members, then this can be interpreted as favoritism. For example, when Maureen died, her son and daughter got together to work on dividing her estate. One afternoon, when they were going through some of her belongings, Maureen's son said to his sister, "You know, I always thought mom favored you." "Why on earth would you think that?" his sister replied. "Because she never stopped talking about you or your kids and telling me what all you were up to, what all you were accomplishing." His sister nearly fell out of her chair. "I felt the same way! Mom always spoke of nothing but you and your kids when she talked to me."

Chapter Seven

- Undermining your grandkids' parents. Your grand-children need consistency, and having the main authority figures in their lives pretty much on the same page on most issues will go a long way towards achieving that goal. This is not to say that you have to agree with their parents on every issue, but what you must take great care to achieve is an awareness and a respect for the lessons and goals that the parents are trying to teach.

- Craving attention. We'll go ahead and put this one out on the table, though we're sure that this is something *you* would never do. The fact is that some grandparents, whether consciously or not, have trouble turning the reins over to the next gen-eration. Maybe they find their empty, quiet house too much to bear and simply need interaction. Whatever the cause, resist the temptation to exag-gerate difficulties, woes, or aches and pains. You may need to shift your focus a bit. Develop interests and activities of your own; it's fine to depend on your family for support, but if you become a con-stant source of difficulty and something is always wrong, you will likely end up driving your family away, psychologically if not physically.

Grandparenting 9-1-1

- Promising more than you can deliver. One grand-mother of ten made the regrettable promise to take each of her grandchildren on a big, exotic trip. She took the oldest to England, then she took two of her grandkids to Hawaii, and then her health began to fail and that was the end of the trips. Seven grandchildren were left feeling cheated, and the reality is that all of the kids were fairly young (under the age of 12), so a trip to the local state fair or the nearby coast would probably have been every bit as much fun for the kids anyway. The grandmother promised too much.

Chapter Seven

In-Law, Out-Law, or Somewhere in Between?

Here's a thorny issue, a wrench in the machinery, a fly in the ointment.... An informal poll of nearly every grandmother we know revealed a common understanding that, for some reason, it is easier to grandparent the children of your daughters than of your sons.

Why? The general consensus seems to be that the relationship with your daughter is usually more relaxed than the relationship with your daughter-in-law. Even those who get along splendidly with their daughters-in-law seem to have a wee bit more trouble in the grandparenting department with the grandkids on this side of the nickel.

There are many possible explanations that can help explain this phenomenon. In most nuclear families, there is a world of subtext and context and shared history that simplifies and lubricates interactions. While you may love your daughter-in-law dearly, the nuclear-family subtext and shared history is, by definition, missing.

This is all assuming that you love your daughter-in-law dearly and wouldn't change a hair on her precious head. But what if you would change her whole head if you could? What if she is, somehow, something less (or more!) than what you had envisioned for your son?

Grandparenting 9-1-1

And, what if you sense that your son and his wife have a somewhat rocky relationship? What if the marriage splits up? What if your daughter-in-law gets primary custody of the kids? What if she moves them across the country to be closer to her family? What will she say to her kids about your son? About *you*?

So, it turns out that there actually is a subtext to this relationship, after all, but it may not be an ideal one for facilitating a close and harmonious relationship.

What to do? What to do?

There is only one place to begin: the daughter-in-law.

Forget the obstacles, forget the subtext, forget the fears, and focus instead on the fact that, for now at least, she is a vital and integral part of your family. Love her in spite of her flaws, just as you love your son in spite of his. (What? He doesn't have any flaws? Ah, we're beginning to get the picture.)

Embark immediately on a crusade to win over the daughter-in-law and to communicate to her that you love her and you love your grandchildren. Begin to build a relationship with her as your relationship with your grandkids grows. Even if the worst happens and they divorce, these will still be your grandchildren, so it is important that you have a solid relationship with your in-law children independent of their spouses.

Chapter Seven

The Ultimate Challenge: Step-Grandparenting

Here it is, what is widely perceived to be the ultimate grandparenting challenge: step-grandparenting. The rules are loose and undefined. What is your role? Where are the boundaries? What is expected of you? What are you supposed to do, what are you supposed to avoid, what can you say and do, what is off limits? And where can you get your own personal copy of the "Official Rules for Step-Grandparents"?

While step-grandparenting is nothing new, the widespread phenomenon of lots of step-grandparents wanting to play a quality, pivotal role in the lives of their inherited offspring is a relatively new phenomenon. There are lots of divorced and now remarried baby boomers out there, and many if not most of them have a step-grandchild or two.

Probably the biggest mistake a new step-grandparent can make is to assume the benefits of the title without first making the requisite investment. A loved, revered grandparent doesn't come by their status overnight, and neither will you.

Instead, approach the new relationship with step-grandchildren with slow, methodical care. Building a relationship takes time, and this relationship is no different. No deference, appreciation, or love will be given automatically.

This is a perfectly understandable and even advisable stance to take on the part of the children. After all, this relationship has come about because a previous relationship failed. Maybe the child lost a grandparent through death. Maybe divorce caused the rift, which leaves the child with the original set of (now separate) grandparents, plus one (or two, if both grandparents remarry).

Grandparenting 9-1-1

The children will naturally view you with caution. Let them. Be yourself, though you may want to ratchet your normally glowing personality down a notch or two. No need in frightening the children unnecessarily!

According to Robert Plofker, co-director of Stepping Stones Family Counseling Center in Ridgewood, New Jersey, step-parents or step-grandparents who try too hard or are too pushy wind up getting frozen out of the family. "It is hoped for that the step-grandparent wants a role, but not a grandparent's role initially. It takes approximately four to seven years for people in blended families to be accepted for who they are," Plofker says.

Take some time to get to know the kids individually. Get down on the floor with the little ones. Ask questions. Be prepared to field questions that may catch you off guard. The children will be curious. You're a novelty, an unknown, a blank slate, and all bets are off.

Most of all, leave any expectations at the door. If you are entertaining thoughts of immediate acceptance and joyous celebration at the mere thought of your presence, forget it. Instead, expect a few sideways glances, a cautionary approach, from a family that has either lost a loved one or been torn apart by divorce. With time and great care you'll eventually be accepted and maybe even loved, but it takes time.

Chapter Seven

"By Any Other Name…"

I am a grandma by default. Excuse me, I need to rephrase—I am a step-grandma by default.

Let me try again; I am part of a grandparenting unit that I entered upon by means of a second marriage to my formerly widowed boyfriend, who has been my husband for the past three years.

If your reaction to this statement is that I am a slave to semantics, then you most likely are not involved in a blended family. For those of us who are, we know that semantics is either the path of diplomacy or the route to familial brouhaha.

I began dating Bob when his middle child was expecting her first child—his first grandchild. Jill and her husband lived far away, across the country. I first met Jill and her beautiful baby girl when they came home for a visit. Kelly was only three months old. By the time Bob and I married two years later, little Kelly was beginning to talk. She called me Patty.

Shortly after our wedding, a second grandchild, Ryan, came along. If one baby could steal your heart, two held your entire mind, body, and soul captive.

Still, I was more than a little hesitant to insert myself into the role of grandma when I had no claim to the name. My heart longed to smother these gorgeous children in my woefully undersized bosom, which ironically reflected my credentials as a grandparent.

I took my concerns to my husband. I asked him how I should engage with the grandchildren without overstepping. I did not want to assume a role that rightly was reserved for another. Nor did I want to be separated from the love or the action because I was not a charter member of the family. I definitely did not want to be viewed as disinterested when in fact I was deeply invested.

Grandparenting 9-1-1

I told Bob I yearned for the luxury of casual acceptance. The kind where you can lavish blatant, biased praise over the smallest achievements without looking like you're pandering, and the right to step in with aged advice of years and experience without appearing like a know-it-all blowhard. I coveted the safety net of ownership.

Bob's wisdom came in the form of a parable. He told me a lovely story about his paternal step-grandfather, Guy. Bob's dad lost his father when he was only fourteen years old. His mother, Gigi, married Guy a few years later. Bob's eyes fairly mist when he speaks of Guy and Gigi. They owned an ice cream store—and who among us would not wish for our grandparents to own an ice cream store!

Beyond spooning dollops of ice cream into Bob's eager mouth, Guy took Bob fishing. Guy baited and hooked not only the fish, but young Bob, too. Guy reeled Bob in with his kind, gentle, and loving spirit. They laughed, joked, and did "guy" things. The only name Guy ever held was Guy, but Bob's heart hears grandpa thirty years after Guy's death.

Bob's story was very comforting to me. I know that gaining acceptance as a new step-grandparent can take time. I can wait. In the meantime my love pours out into their open willing spirits in spurts, sometimes gushing forth, other times more measured, but always wholesome and pure.

Then when the time comes, and in my best grandma fashion—as all good grandmas do—I will relate a multitude of family stories to Kelly and Ryan and the nameless wonders of future step-grandchildren and grandchildren. My wish is that all the "grands" will be cousins-in-arms gathered around the sprightly little old woman (me) while she weaves her tales.

Chapter Seven

And the first story I will tell will be this: One day not too long ago, in a city far away, four-year-old Kelly was happily chatting to her mom when her mother mentioned something about Grandpa. Kelly asked for clarification; my grandpa with grandma, or my grandpa with my Patty?

At this point in the storytelling I will pause to ask, "How do you like that? I am Kelly's Patty!" I will shout these words with tremendous animation by flinging my arms wide open as if to embrace the world, throwing my head back, giggling in delight, kicking my bare feet into the air and wiggling my toes. I will proclaim to all the children of the generation two steps down from mine that the possessive "my" followed by whatever name that comes to mind creates a glorious state of being.

—**Contributed by Patty Swyden Sullivan**

Grandparenting 9-1-1

Effective Grandparenting When You're Sick

Some of the most valuable lessons that grandparents teach involve large, difficult issues of illness and death. Illness has a way of stripping life of its fluff and revealing the issues and people and matters that are truly significant. Just as grandchildren learn valuable lessons about life from their grandparents, they also learn valuable lessons about illness and death from them.

The amount of grandparenting you can do when you're sick depends on the nature and severity of the illness. Your relationship with your grandkids will be different if you suffer from chronic illness than if you have to deal with an intense, short-term illness and recovery.

If you are chronically ill, look for ways to interact with your grandchildren that don't tax your already-compromised health. It may be unrealistic to plan an all-day outing hiking around the zoo, though you may be able to take them on a short picnic instead, where you can enjoy them from your seat beneath a shade tree.

Maybe packing a picnic is even a bit of a stretch. You can save your energy further by driving through McDonald's and picking up a lunch to take to the park. The goal here is to figure out ways to do fun things with the grandkids that they will enjoy and that are doable for you.

Another good way to spend an afternoon: take the kids to a movie. Once you get there, all you have to do is sit in a darkened theater with them for an hour or two, and what you gain in return is a common experience that you can call upon later. "Wasn't it fun to watch the little mermaid swim away from Ursula, the evil octopus?"

Chapter Seven

If you are very sick and housebound, possibly even bedridden, play an occasional board game, scratch out a few games of Tic Tac Toe, read books together, work a crossword puzzle, or just snuggle in bed and watch a favorite show. Let the kids make popcorn and bring it to bed with you. You can interact with your mind even when your body isn't cooperating.

The benefits of having your grandchildren nearby when you are sick shouldn't be underestimated. Grandchildren can make you laugh, and they can help take your mind off your physical discomfort and help you focus on something else.

The presence of grandchildren can also provide comfort on a deeper level. It is gratifying to watch the next generation, flush with health, and to observe the circle of life continuing. While these aren't easy issues to deal with, they can be deeply satisfying. Even if you are gravely ill, you can observe your brood around you and feel gratified at what you have helped create. This—your family, your children, your grandchildren—is likely the most lasting element of your life's work. Enjoy the time you spend with them and value them for the joy they can bring to your life.

Communicating effectively with your kids and grandkids when you are sick may take on new meaning. Maybe your life before you became ill revolved around playing bridge with your friends; maybe now you have lost interest in that old pastime and want to spend more time with your family instead. Talk to your grandchildren about this shift in perspective; this is how they learn.

Grandparenting 9-1-1

When Jeanine, the mother of two and grandmother of four, was first diagnosed with cancer, she accepted the diagnosis with steely resolve and grace. She was determined to help her family as much as she could, while she was able. One of her granddaughters, Blaine, came to spend a week with her, and together they sifted through boxes of old family photographs, carefully noting names on the back. Jeanine wanted to make sure her knowledge of the family wasn't lost when she died.

While her care of family records was admirable, what was even more important during that time was the strength she demonstrated to her then-teenage granddaughter. Blaine was amazed by the calm determination she saw in her grandmother, the brave and uncomplaining way she dealt with pain, and her focus on accomplishing something she thought was important before it was too late.

"In that week I spent with my grandmother, she gave me recipes, told me the stories behind various objects in her house, and even gave me the gloves she wore to her wedding, which she had tucked away in a corner of her closet. Those gloves are now among my most prized possessions, but if we hadn't spent that time together they would have been lost—no one would have realized what they were.

"We were close before, but during that week I felt such a strong connection with her, and I know she felt it, too," says Blaine. "I know it sounds corny, but I really believe that for years and years my grandmother showed me how to live, and then, in the end, she showed me how to die. I love her for that, for being real and honest with me during the most difficult time of her life."

Chapter Seven

Although it may be difficult, as much as possible try to minimize the physical discomfort you feel. Your grandchildren will know you are sick; this is frightening knowledge in and of itself. As much as you are able, cast the illness in a long-term perspective: I'm sick now, but I had many wonderful years of health.

This can also be a prime opportunity to communicate the importance of making good health-related decisions. If you smoked for years and now suffer from emphysema, use this fact to teach your grandkids about the importance of avoiding cigarettes. Your family will not think less of you for acknowledging past mistakes.

Grandparenting 9-1-1

Building a Legacy

"With every deed you are sowing a seed, though the harvest you may not see."

—Ella Wheeler Wilcox

In this book we have examined practical ways of spending time with your grandchildren, and we have seen how a strong intergenerational relationship benefits both children and adults. Not every idea will suit every lifestyle or temperament, but we hope you will pick and choose from the ideas we have presented, with the end goal of strengthening and improving your relationships with your grandchildren.

As you work to build these relationships, keep in mind that there are other, more lasting results as well. Your memory, the things you believe in, the lessons you teach, and the time you spend selflessly will all be remembered by your children, grandchildren and, if you're lucky, great-grandchildren, long after your time on earth is over.

The lessons you teach and the legacy you leave will not likely be fully realized for years to come. Your strength of character, honesty, and recipe for chocolate pie have the potential to live long after you're gone, if you take the time and effort to pass along what you know and care about to your family.

It is the wise grandparent who realizes that good, strong relationships don't happen by accident. If you invest your time and energy into these most vital, young, impressionable people—your grandchildren—you will enjoy years of friendship, companionship, and admiration, and your legacy will be durable and strong.

"And now I have finished a work that neither the wrath of love, nor fire, nor the sword, nor devouring age shall be able to destroy."

—Ovid (43 B.C.-A.D. 18)

Appendix

Book List

A Classic Reading Guide for Grandparents

0–18 months

Board books are great for this age.

Goodnight, Moon — Margaret Wise Brown
  Always a favorite bedtime book.

Runaway Bunny — Margaret Wise Brown
  A cuddly and loving little book.

Big Red Barn — Margaret Wise Brown
  Sleepy time for the animals.

The Very Hungry Caterpillar — Eric Carle
  So hungry he eats a hole through the pictures in the book!

Mr. Brown Can Moo, Can You — Dr. Seuss
  Dr. Seuss's book of wonderful noises.

Appendix

Hand, Hand, Finger, Thumb — Al Perkins
  A rhythm book for little ones.

A Child's Garden of Verses — Robert Louis Stevenson
  Beloved children's classic.

More More More Said the Baby — Vera Williams
  Three love stories for babies and young children.

ABC — Brian Wildsmith

Tomie's Little Mother Goose — Tomie dePaola
  A lovely introduction to Mother Goose.

The Wheels on the Bus — Jerry Smith
  Based on the popular children's song.

Off Your Rocker!
The Ultimate Guide for Grandparents

Appendix

18 months–3 years

Do You Want to Be My Friend? — Eric Carle
  Each page has the end of an animal's tail, and the child guesses which animal.

A Boy, A Dog, A Frog — Mercer Mayer
  An entertaining picture book for young ones.

Chicka Chicka Boom Boom —
  Bill Martin, Jr. and John Archambault

Guess How Much I Love You — Sam McBratney
  A comforting tale of love.

* *The Bag I'm Taking to Grandma's* — Shirley Neitzel

Have You Seen My Duckling? — Nancy Tafuri
  Discover the hidden ducklings on each page.

I Love You, Little One — Nancy Tafuri
  A book of bedtime assurance.

* Includes Grandparents.

Appendix

Sylvia Long's Mother Goose — Sylvia Long

Mother Goose — Tomie dePaola
Charming illustrations distinguish this one.

Animal Seasons — Brian Wildsmith

Corduroy's Day — Don Freeman
A good board book for toddlers.

Over the Hills and Far Away — Alan Marks
This author presents an exquisitely illustrated collection of sixty classic Mother Goose rhymes.

Is It Time? — Marilyn Janovitz
A funny, rhythmic bedtime book featuring father and son wolves.

Five Little Ducks — Pamela Paparone
One by one, the little ducks go over the hills and far away in this traditional rhyme, transformed by artist Pamela Paparone into a simple counting book for very young children.

Appendix

3–5 years

Oh My Baby, Little One — Kathi Appelt
Celebrating the bond of love that holds family
members together, despite the distances that
sometimes separate them.

Little Toot — Hardie Gramatky
An old favorite. A mischievous tugboat
saves the day.

* *The Napping House* — Audrey Wood
A grandma and her grandson fall asleep on a rainy
day… and chaos results!

Make Way for Ducklings — Robert McCloskey
Mrs. Mallard and her ducklings stop traffic
in Boston. McCloskey's books are delightful
to children.

Ask Mr. Bear — Marjorie Flack

Mike Mulligan and His Steam Shovel — Virginia Burton
Mike and his steam shovel race against time
to dig a cellar.

* Includes Grandparents.

Appendix

A Hole Is to Dig: A Book of First Definitions
— Ruth Krauss
Active definitions for preschoolers, such as "Hands are to hold."

Best Word Book Ever — Richard Scarry
Full of detailed pictures toddlers love.

The Tale of Peter Rabbit — Beatrix Potter
Miniature books with characters you'll want to meet and sensitive illustrations.

Curious George — Hans Rey
This funny little monkey wins the hearts of his myriad fans. Twenty books in the series.

Perrault's Complete Fairy Tales — Charles Perrault
Contains some of the best known fairy tales in Western literature, such as *Cinderella* and *Little Red Riding Hood.*

Side by Side: Poems to Read Together
— Collected by Lee Bennett Hopkins
Traditional and contemporary poems to read aloud to young children. Covers seasons, holidays, animals, and lullabies.

Off Your Rocker!
The Ultimate Guide for Grandparents

Appendix

The Cat in the Hat — Dr. Seuss
Dr. Seuss's wacky books are fun for experiencing language and rhymes.

Corduroy — Don Freeman
The adventures of a teddy bear who lives in a toy store.

If You Give a Mouse a Cookie — Laura Numeroff
A funny tale of sequential actions.

If You Take a Mouse to the Movies — Laura Numeroff
The energetic mouse is busy again.

Little Bear — Else Holmelund Minarik
Poignant little stories about a child-bear and his family.

* *What's under My Bed?* — James Stevenson
In this series, a grandfather concocts tales about his childhood to sooth the fears of his grandchildren.

Poems and Prayers for the Very Young
— Martha Alexander

The Fairy Tale Treasury
— Collected by Virginia Haviland
Popular tales from Grimm, Anderson, and Perrault with full-color art.

* Includes Grandparents.

Appendix

5–7 years

(Beginning Readers)

* *The Berenstain Bears and the Giddy Grandma*
  — Stan and Jan Berenstain

* *Cloudy with a Chance of Meatballs* — Judi Barrett
  A hilarious story told by a grandpa about meals pouring down from the sky.

Grandfather Counts
  A Chinese grandfather comes to live with his American daughter and grandchildren, and they begin to learn about different languages, cultures, and each other.

* *Nana Upstairs and Nana Downstairs*
  — Tomie dePaola
  Two stores about assisting aging family members.

* *My Little Artist* — Donna Green
  Artistic grandmother passes that heritage on to her granddaughter.

* *Miss Fannie's Hat* — Jan Karon
  The author based this story on her wonderful hat-loving grandmother.

* *Granddaddy's Gift* — Margaree King Mitchell
  The story of freedom for a young African American grandchild.

* Includes Grandparents.

Appendix

* *Twice Yours, A Parable of God's Gift* — Nan Gurley
  A grandfather relates to his grandson a gentle story that applies to what God has done for us.

* *Thundercakes* — Patricia Polacco
  A little girl's grandmother helps her overcome her fear of thunder.

Clifford the Big Red Dog — Norman Bridwell
  A delightful series of books that teaches valuable lessons and entertains at the same time.

Birds — Brian Wildsmith

Best Read-It-Yourself Book Ever — Richard Scarry
  Entertaining stories for new readers.

Madeline — Ludwig Bemelmans
  A delightful series about a daring and adventuresome little French girl and her friends. She has delighted generations of readers in the early grades.

Alexander and the Terrible, Horrible, No Good, Very Bad Day — Judith Viorst
  Alexander has the worst bad day of all.

* Includes Grandparents.

Appendix

Where the Wild Things Are — Maurice Sendak
Amazingly, children love Sendak's fantasy about a little boy and the monsters that haunt all children.

The Sleepy Book — Charlotte Zolotow
Perfect reading for bedtime.

Uncle Jed's Barbershop — Margaree King Mitchell
A lifelong dream achieved at the grand age of seventy-nine!

Through Moon and Stars and Night Skies
— Ann Turner
The tender story of an adopted child's trip across the sea to meet his new parents.

A Chair for My Mother — Vera B. Williams
The story of a child who sacrifices for a hardworking mother.

George and Martha — James Marshall
Back in print! Kids love these two fat, friendly hippos.

Appendix

7–9 years

* *My Island Grandma* — Kathryn Lasky
  Special summer times between a little girl and her grandmother.

* *Grandpa's Soup* — Eiko Kadono
  Grandpa discovers a good cure for his loneliness and sadness over Grandma's death.

Amelia Bedelia — Peggy Paris
  Amelia, the new maid, takes everything literally with silly results. There are a number of enjoyable sequels.

Aesops' Fables — Aesop
  Ancient stories with a moral teach timeless truths.

The Chronicles of Narnia — C. S. Lewis
  This series of seven books contains fantasy enjoyed by grownups as well as children.

Winnie the Pooh — A. A. Milne
  Children are delighted by this lovable bear and his friends, including Piglet, Tigger, and Eeyore.

* Includes Grandparents.

Appendix

The Magic Tree House Series — Mary Pope Osborne
The magical adventures of Annie and Jack interest even reluctant learners in reading.

The Best Christmas Pageant Ever — Barbara Robinson
The rowdiest family takes over the church Christmas pageant.

The Courage of Sarah Noble — Alice Dalgliesh
Tells the story of a brave eight-year-old girl at the beginning of the eighteenth century. Based on a true incident in the colonial wilderness.

The Story of Holly and Ivy — Rumer Godden
Unforgettable story of a lonely, runaway orphan girl, an unsold Christmas doll, and a childless couple.

The Velveteen Rabbit — Margery Williams
A beloved toy rabbit becomes real through the love that a little boy bestows on him.

Charlotte's Web — E. B. White
This highly acclaimed classic addresses the cycle of life tenderly through the tale of a young girl who loves animals and a pig who needs a friend.

Appendix

Homer Price — Robert McCloskey
> The neighborhood dilemmas encountered by this small-town boy will keep you laughing.

James and the Giant Peach — Roald Dahl
> James, an orphan, must live with his mean aunts. See what happens when a giant peach full of characters begins to grow in the backyard. An absolute favorite of many.

Mr. Brown and Mr. Gray — William Wondriska
> A story that explores contentment versus greed as two pigs, Mr. Brown and Mr. Gray, experience having all they want for a year. Humor along with emphasis on important values.

Off Your Rocker!
The Ultimate Guide for Grandparents

Appendix

9–12 years

Little House on the Prairie — Laura Ingalls Wilder
Part of a series of stories about the Ingalls family. Wonderful reading, full of warmth and the adventure of pioneer days.

Abraham Lincoln — Ingri and Edgar D'Aulaire
The life of Lincoln from his boyhood through his presidency is beautifully written and illustrated. Also look for their biographies of Washington, Franklin, and Columbus.

The Secret Garden — Frances Hodgson Burnett
In this longtime favorite, a little girl changes the life of her cousin and the other members of a joyless Victorian household.

Harriet the Spy — Louise Fitzhugh
Harriet's practice of spying on others and writing about them in her notebook results in her becoming an outcast and learning an important lesson.

The Jungle Book — Rudyard Kipling
Timeless, imaginative stories of jungle animals.

Call It Courage — Armstrong Sperry
A Polynesian boy finds the courage to face his fears and a raging sea.

Appendix

The Bridge to Terabithia — Katherine Paterson
> Two young friends enjoy a secret kingdom named Terabithia. One dies, leaving the other to learn how to go on after such loss.

My Side of the Mountain — Jean Craighead George
> A modern-day Robinson Crusoe in which a young boy learns to survive and live with nature.

From the Mixed-Up Files of Mrs. Basil E. Frankweiler — E.L. Konigsburg
> A mystery featuring two children who run away to live at the Metropolitan Museum of Art.

* *Sun and Spoon* — Kevin Henkes
> Spoon's discussions with his grandfather after his grandmother's death help him understand what made his grandparents' relationship so special.

* *Heidi* — Johanna Spyri
> A beautiful story of a girl, her grandfather, and a boy named Peter. Set in the mountains of Switzerland.

Dobry — Monica Shannon
> Through this lovely story of family life in Bulgaria, you will be aided in seeing, feeling, and loving.

* Includes Grandparents.

Appendix

King of the Wind — Marguerite Henry
> An unforgettable horse story that still pleases readers.

Henry Huggins — Beverly Cleary
> An enjoyable series of the adventures of Henry, his dog Ribsy, and their friends.

Where the Red Fern Grows — Wilson Rawls
> Poignant story of how a young boy gets the pair of coon hounds he wants and what they mean to him. Requires tissues!

The Wolves of Willoughby Chase — Joan Aiken
> A great English estate, a wicked governess, lots of romance, adventure, and melodrama.

The Wind in the Willows — Kenneth Grahame
> A tale of the adventures of beloved characters Mole, Rat, Badger, and Toad. It's ageless.

Caddie Woodlawn — Carol Ryrie Brink
> Follow the adventures of Caddie, an impulsive and brave tomboy, during pioneer days in Wisconsin. A long-beloved story.

Tales from Shakespeare — Charles and Mary Lamb
> A good introduction to Shakespeare, with plots condensed and written in good story form.

Off Your Rocker!

Appendix

Anthologies

Classics to Read Aloud to Your Children
— William Russell
A compilation of selections of the best from
poetry, fairy tales, short stories, and novels. The
works are divided into three levels of listening,
beginning with ages five to seven.

More Classics to Read Aloud to Your Children
— William Russell
Another marvelous collection of great stories,
poems, and excerpts from novels and plays,
spanning centuries and styles. Also divided into
listening levels five and up, eight and up, and
eleven and up. Entertainment for reader as well
as listener.

The Children's Book of Virtues
— Edited by William Bennett
Wonderful stories that illustrate virtues that are
the essentials of good character. An ideal story-
book to help lead young minds toward what is
noble, gentle, and fine.

Eric Carle's Treasury of Classic Stories for Children
— Eric Carle
Stories from Grimm, Andersen, and Aesop,
accompanied by colorful collages.

Appendix

Sing a Song of Popcorn: Every Child's Book of Poems
— Beatrice Schenk deRegniers
Outstanding sounds and sights, with illustrations by nine Caldecott Medal artists.

Where the Sidewalk Ends — Shel Silverstein
The best-loved collection of poetry for children, with such titles as "Crocodile's Toothache" and "If I Had a Brontosaurus."

A Light in the Attic — Shel Silverstein
The second children's book to make the New York Times best-seller list, where it remained for 186 weeks.

NOTES

NOTES

Off Your Rocker!
The Ultimate Guide for Grandparents

NOTES